MINDFULNESS
In A Messed Up World

*A Mindfulness Workbook to
Reduce Anxiety, Relieve Stress & Stop Overthinking
—
Simple, No-Nonsense Exercises to Calm Your Mind
& Regulate Your Nervous System*

Disclaimer:
This book is for educational, informational, and entertainment purposes only. It is not intended to diagnose, treat, cure, or prevent any physical or mental health condition. Always consult a qualified medical or mental health professional before applying any techniques described.

The author and publisher make no guarantees regarding results and disclaim any liability for any outcomes resulting from the use of this material.

About the Series
The I CAN'T AFFORD THERAPY series is **not** anti-therapy. Therapy can be incredibly valuable, and if you have access to it, it's always worth considering. This book is designed for those who may not currently have that option and are looking for practical tools in the meantime.

This book is not a substitute for professional care, but it's a practical starting point when support isn't accessible.

Quotations & Sources: Every effort has been made to credit the sources of quotes and ideas used. Any unintentional omission will be corrected in future editions upon request.

Trademarks: All trademarks, product names, company names, and logos are the property of their respective owners.

Illustrations by LifeZen Publications
ISBN 9789083575452 (Paperback)

Let's be honest...

Often, no matter how much we try, the mind just doesn't switch off.

We overthink everything.
We replay conversations.
We feel anxious for no clear reason.
We try to relax—but our brains won't let us.

And the world around us?
It's loud. Fast. Messed up.

So when someone says "practice mindfulness," or "try to relax," or "just tune it out."
It feels unrealistic.

Because in moments like this, the problem isn't understanding the idea.

It's finding something that actually works.

This book isn't about *thinking* differently.
It's about *doing* something different.

This workbook includes:

- 60+ guided exercises for anxiety, stress, and overthinking.
- Mindfulness practices that fit naturally into everyday life.
- Short, simple calming techniques you can use anytime.
- Body-based methods to calm your nervous system settle, reset, and feel safe.
- Gentle ways to create space between your thoughts and your reactions.

You don't need to be "good at mindfulness."
You just need to **start**.

Try This First…

Exercise: Calm Your Mind in 60 Seconds

Take a slow breath in through your nose (4 seconds).
Hold gently (2 seconds).
Exhale slowly through your mouth (6 seconds).

Repeat 3 times.

Now notice:

- Your forehead
- Your shoulders
- Your jaw
- Your breathing

Awesome.

That small shift you just felt?
That's where this workbook begins.

You don't need to fix everything at once.
You just need small moments like this.

That's how your mind begins to slow down.
That's how your body begins to relax.
That's how you stay steady—even in a messy world.

Table of Contents

A Mindful Gift for You

Enjoy your **bonus guided meditations and affirmations**, created to gently support your mindfulness journey at https://life-zen.com/bonus/mindfulness Or scan the QR code on this page to listen.

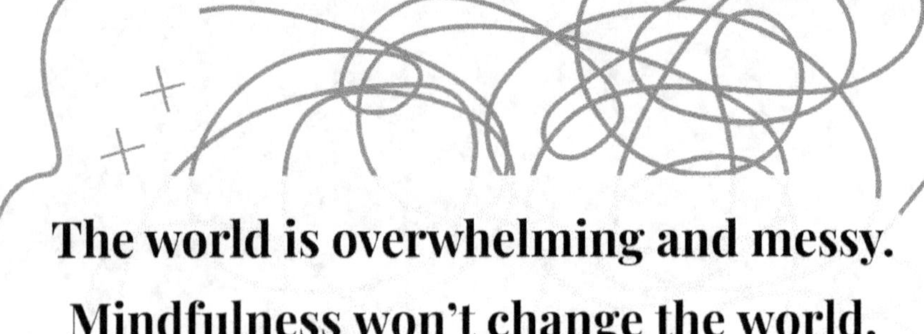

The world is overwhelming and messy.
Mindfulness won't change the world.
But it can make you steady inside it.
– LifeZen

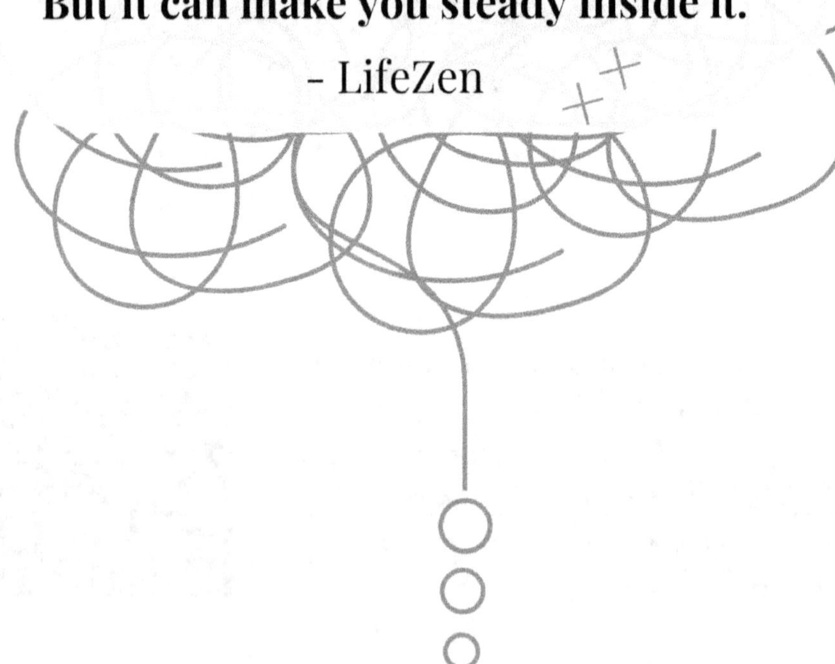

Introduction

The first time I tried mindfulness... I gave up.

I couldn't quiet my mind, I was fidgety, and my thoughts were jumping from one to the next. *What time is it? How long have I been sitting here? What's for dinner? I really should be doing something else...*

So, I stood up and pretty much thought mindfulness was a waste of time. *(And if you've ever felt the same way, this workbook is for you.)*

But I'm also a person of reason. I was aware of all the science behind the positive effects of mindfulness, so I'd give it a try now and then. Until one day, a thought popped into my head *while* I was trying to be quiet (and not being successful at it).

I thought, *"Wow, if I can't control my own mind and chill out for sixty seconds, how am I functioning throughout the day? Who's actually in control?"*

That thought unsettled me a bit, so I tried to dig deeper.

If I wasn't directing my mind... then what (or who) the heck was? *Habits? Stress? Deadlines? My phone? Old fears? Mom..?!*

I always considered myself to be self-aware and intentional. But sitting there, unable to do even a few mindful breaths without mentally wandering off, what did that say about the rest of my day?

How many decisions was I making "without thinking?"
What am I NOT noticing around me because I'm rushing?
How often was I reacting instead of responding?

Reacting vs. Responding
Reacting is automatic. Responding is intentional.

Reacting: *something happens, and you immediately act from emotion, habit, or impulse. There's no space in between. It's fast, and often later you think, "I wish I hadn't said that."*

Responding: *something happens, and you pause, even briefly. You notice what you're feeling. You consider your options. And then you choose what to say or do.*

I started paying closer attention.

And what I noticed wasn't dramatic or spiritual. It was pretty ordinary, really. *(But then again, the "simple and ordinary" have this annoying way of being truly what matters, right?)*

One of the first things I noticed was that **whenever I went out with friends to "relax and decompress," I couldn't sleep that night.** It's like I was even more high-strung.

I would replay full-on conversations in my head. Actually, that's not true, I wasn't just replaying them, I was... *rewriting* them.

I would go over what *they* said, what *I* said, and I would just sort of... continue the conversation in my head. Oh, I should have said, "A', then they might have said "B," and then I would say, "C." On and on it went.

Honestly, for a while, I thought something was wrong with me. *(Why was I doing this? Why can't I let it go? Why the excessive post-event processing?!)*

But as I got deeper into mindfulness, I learned that this is something many people experience. It's a common mental pattern.

The mind continues to process—replaying, analyzing, and attempting to resolve or redo things—even when the moment is already over. It's as if the mind is trying to close a "loop," because something feels unfinished. (In reality, it's because we feel that something is disappointing or unsatisfactory.)

And that's when I noticed something else: I couldn't step out of my own thoughts. Like most people, **my mind was constantly moving between two places: the past and the future.**

The PAST was about replaying and reliving what happened.

In addition to rewriting social conversations with my friends... I noticed I was spending A LOT of time in my past. Not intentionally. A memory would surface, and suddenly I was back there.

And while there's nothing wrong with reminiscing, my mind didn't usually go to the good moments. It often drifted toward the unpleasant ones. And before I knew it, I was feeling sad, sometimes devastated... over something I could no longer change.

The FUTURE was about worrying and trying to plan what may happen next.

I noticed that my mind was constantly planning, anticipating, overthinking, and trying to solve problems that may or may not happen. Even when nothing urgent was going on, there was this low-level hum of mental noise running in the background inside me.

So, I spend a lot of time and energy in the PAST and the FUTURE. Where the heck was "**NOW**"? Where was the present moment?

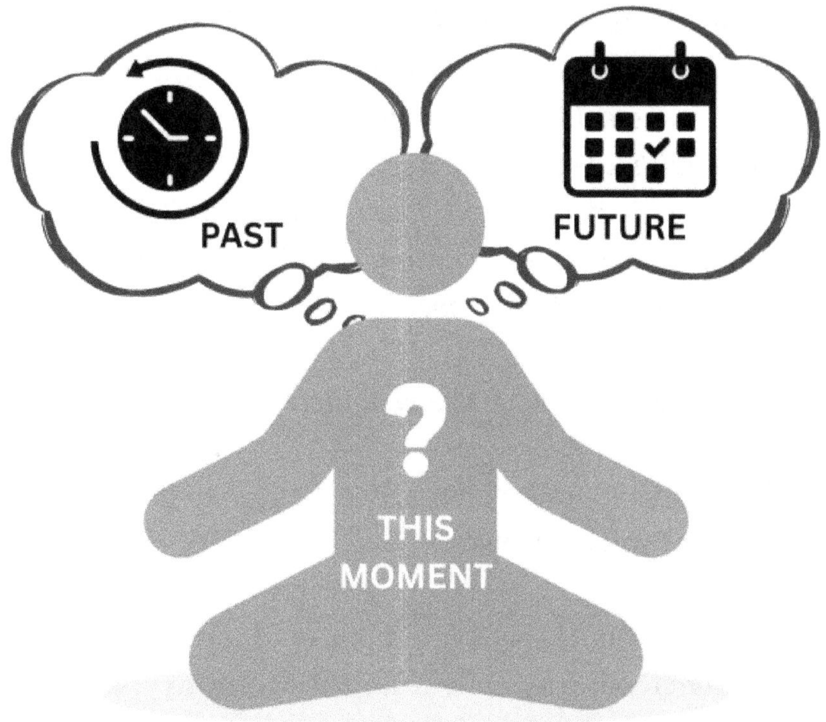

And that's what finally made me try mindfulness in earnest: the realization that I was always missing "now."

Mind you, mindfulness didn't suddenly make my racing thoughts disappear. But it slowly showed me that I didn't have to pursue every single one of them. I didn't have to "pull at the string" of every thought I had.

In the end, I realized that mindfulness wasn't about forcing my mind to be quiet. It wasn't about sitting perfectly still or achieving some peaceful, blank, Zen state either. It was about **noticing**.

Noticing what my mind was doing.
Noticing what my body was feeling.
Noticing how quickly I got pulled into stress, irritation, or distraction without even realizing it.
Noticing who had so much "power" over me that a single comment, delayed reply, or even a certain look or tone of voice could completely shift my mood.

And that shift in awareness changed more than I expected.

Over time, and with repeated practice, I began to understand the **real value of mindfulness**.

It wasn't just about taking a few minutes to relax or calm down. It was about creating a kind of **mental sanctuary, a place of safety inside myself** I could return to, no matter what was happening around me.

And from that place, something unexpected started to grow: **resilience**.

Not the forced, "just push through it" kind, but a steadier force. It's the ability to:

- Feel stress without being swallowed by it
- Experience strong emotions without having them dictate my actions
- Recall a memory without getting pulled back into it or reliving the emotions attached to it

- Move through this messy, loud, unpredictable, and often scary world without constantly losing my footing

Mindfulness didn't make life quieter. It made me steadier inside it. It's my hope you will achieve the same in this book.

How to Use this Workbook

Mindfulness can sometimes feel... abstract. You hear about being "present," noticing your thoughts, or calming your mind, but when you try it, the question becomes: ***What exactly am I supposed to do?***

That's why I designed this workbook this way.

Rather than simply explaining mindfulness, this book helps you practice it. The goal isn't just to understand the ideas, but to experience them in real life. Each chapter introduces a concept in a simple, practical way, and then gives you exercises to help you apply it to your own thoughts, habits, and daily situations.

So, the worksheets are not there for decoration.
They're where the real work happens!

Over time, these small moments of awareness start to add up. You may notice that you react less impulsively, feel less overwhelmed by racing thoughts, and recover more quickly from stressful situations. You may begin to experience a little more space between what happens around you and how you respond to it.

And with practice, that *space* can become a steady point of calm and clarity, even in the middle of today's busy, messy, and unpredictable world.

Ava Watters

Amazon International Bestselling Author
Survivor

Part 1: Why Your Mind Won't Slow Down (Even If You Want It To)

Chapter 1: The World is LOUD

Nowadays, the world seems a lot noisier, scarier, messier. Why is that?

I think it's because "input" right now has dramatically increased. Here's just one small example: a few decades ago, news arrived at set times. You get the morning paper, and then settle down at night to consume the evening news. There was a natural pause, a gap in between information consumption.

Today, we are updated on everything—big or small, important or irrelevant—all the effing time!

Although that didn't happen overnight, it still happened too fast. Stress escalated before we even realized what was happening. And then one day, we woke up and thought, *"Why am I so tired and stressed out?!"*

When your mental bandwidth is constantly stretched, even small things start to feel BIG. A minor inconvenience feels personal. A simple decision feels exhausting. A short delay feels irritating.

Feeling this way is NOT because you're weak or incapable. It's because your system is overloaded. And this is exactly where mindfulness becomes relevant.

You see, **mindfulness is a way of protecting your attention in a world that's constantly trying to take it.**

It's a way for you to create small pauses in a culture that has quietly erased them.

But before we talk about *how* to do that, you need to understand what you're up against.

Digital Overload

Would you believe that just 30 years ago, there were none of these?

- Notifications.
- Push alerts.
- Group chats buzzing at midnight.
- Breaking news banners flashing across screens.
- Unread message counters.
- Endless scrolling feeds.
- Email inboxes filling up while you sleep.

The modern world runs on **constant input**, and we rarely experience this input as neutral. We interpret it as dramatic. Urgent. Emotional.

Even when it isn't really urgent, it feels like it is! *(Be honest. When you get a notification, can you ignore it and not pick up your phone? Can you put off replying to someone who just texted you? Even if you don't reply, you'll probably be drafting your answer in your head, right?)*

And what about the 24/7 news cycle? If something happens anywhere in the world, you know about it within *seconds*. And it's not just information. It's emotionally charged information. Crisis. Conflict. Disaster. Outrage.

Unfortunately, **humans are not designed to process this volume of information**. Evolution shaped our nervous system for a very different environment. It operates, in simple terms, like an "on" and "off" switch.

You receive input. Your brain scans for threat.
And if something feels uncertain, intense, or potentially dangerous, your nervous system switches to "On."

"On" then triggers an increase in your heart rate, a tightening in your muscles, a narrowing of your focus, and the flush of stress hormones all throughout your body.

This response is incredibly useful *if* you're facing real and immediate danger. If a predator appears, you want that surge of energy. You want to be alert, fast, and ready for action.

But here's the problem: **the brain doesn't differentiate very well between a physical threat and a psychological one**. A simple, annoying email can activate the same stress pathway as a sudden loud noise.

And then, before you can settle down, another "threat alert" arrives, such as someone *not* replying to your SMS message.

Individually, these inputs seem small. Collectively, they fragment your focus, hijack your emotions, and trigger you all day long.

Even when you put your phone on mute or silent, your mind isn't really switched off for notifications. A small part of you is still on standby... half-waiting, half-listening, maybe even half-hoping. That's low-level ongoing anticipation.

So this is what digital overload has done to you. You got attuned to constant micro-interruptions that prevent your mind from ever fully settling.

No wonder you feel physically tired and mentally exhausted. Your attention never slows down or rests.

The "Hurry Sickness"

Do you ever feel guilty when you're not productive? Many people feel this way. I sure did.

Somewhere along the way, being busy became a badge of honor. If you ask someone how they're doing, the answer is often, *"Busy."* And it's said with a strange mix of fatigue and pride.

Productivity has become tied to identity. If you're not doing, achieving, optimizing, improving... then what *are* you doing?

That's why taking a break and resting feels uncomfortable, even irresponsible for some. You sit down to relax, and within minutes, you think: *"I really should be doing _______?"*

You finish one task, and instead of feeling even a sliver of satisfaction, your mind jumps to... *next!* There's always more: more emails; more deadlines; more appointments (business and personal), more goals; more catching up. More everything.

Some psychologists call this the **hurry sickness**, which is characterized by constant internal rush, even when there's no actual emergency.[1,2] For example:

- You call someone *while* standing in line.
- You scroll your phone *while* watching a show.
- You listen to an audiobook *while* cooking.
- You add to your To-Do list *while* talking to someone.

Some people may characterize this as being productive or a great multitasker. But in this mode, slowing down can feel almost threatening. As if pausing means falling behind, but falling behind what?

Often, it's not a real deadline. It's an *internalized standard*, a belief that your worth is linked to your output. So even when the external noise quiets, the internal pressure keeps building.

Your Brain vs. the Modern World

Human brains evolved in a very different environment. For most of human history, our ancestors lived in small groups and dealt with immediate, local problems. Our nervous systems were also built to handle short bursts of stress followed by recovery.

A predator appears → adrenaline spikes → you run → you survive → your body calms down.

But what you experience today is different.

Instead of short bursts of real physical danger, you face constant psychological stimulation. You receive hundreds of tiny "threats" daily in the form of social comparison, negative headlines, work demands, financial worries, performance pressure, etc.

And unlike a real predator, these modern-day stressors don't resolve quickly; they linger. As a result, your nervous system stays slightly activated. It's not enough to trigger panic, but it's enough to keep you wired.

On top of that, your brain is drawn to novelty.[3] New information equals potential survival value. So when you refresh your feed or check a notification, your brain rewards you with a small hit of dopamine.

Bottom-line: You're running ancient hardware on modern software. And the scale is the problem.

You're exposed to *more* people in a single day online than your ancestors met in a lifetime. That means *more* opinions, *more* comparisons, *more* expectations, *more* drama, more *crises*, and so on.

And yet... You (or others around you) expect yourself to feel calm, focused, and emotionally steady all the time. When you understand this huge mismatch, something shifts.

You stop seeing your overwhelm as a personal failure, and start seeing it as a predictable response to a messy world.

Does this mean you're trapped? Does this mean there's nothing you can do? Absolutely not.

The world may be loud—digitally, socially, culturally, psychologically—but you can learn how to step *outside* of that noise.

That's where mindfulness comes in.

Mindfulness isn't an escape from the noise. It's not a way of pretending the world isn't chaotic or "stepping out" of reality. It's a way of staying steady inside it.

Note: The following exercises (Worksheets 1-3) invite you to slow down and do a bit of *noticing* about your life. If that feels like too much right now, that's okay. You can skip them for now and return when you feel more comfortable.

Exercise 1: Where Is the "Noise" Coming From?

Before you try to change anything, let's simply notice what's competing for your attention and energy. This exercise isn't about judging your life. It's about seeing it clearly.

Step 1: Daily Demands

Write down everything that regularly asks something of you. **Tip:** Think of how your day goes. What activities or situations take up most of your time?

Work:

Examples: attending meetings, replying to emails and messages, managing my team

____

____

____

____

____

Home / Family:

Examples: planning meals, cooking, coordinating schedules

____

____

____

____

____

Health / Personal:

Examples: trying to exercise consistently, keeping up with personal admin (insurance, paperwork, appointments)

____

____

____

____

____

Ongoing Responsibilities That Never Feel "Done":

Examples: caring for elderly parents, seeing to a child with special needs, managing a household, etc.

____

____

____

____

____

Step 2: Digital Input

Which ones consume most of your time and energy?

- ☐ Social media scrolling
- ☐ Frequent notifications
- ☐ Checking email multiple times a day
- ☐ Group chats
- ☐ News updates
- ☐ Work apps
- ☐ Others:

____

____

Reflect:

When during the day do you feel most digitally overloaded?

____

Example: All day, really. During the day at work, and when I come home, I "unwind" by scrolling online.

____

____

____

____

Step 3: Mental Carryover

What stays in your mind even when the day is technically "over"?

- ☐ Unfinished work
- ☐ Conversations replaying
- ☐ Tasks I forgot
- ☐ Worries about tomorrow
- ☐ Small irritations that happened
- ☐ Annoying news
- ☐ Irritating comments I read online
- ☐ Others:

____

____

Step 4: Pause & Notice

Looking at the lists above, where is most of the "noise" coming from?

- ☐ Work
- ☐ Home
- ☐ Myself
- ☐ The World Around Me

☐ Others:

____

____

Now gently ask yourself: *Is this noise coming from external demands... or from internal pressure?*

For example:
- Expectations I place on myself
- The need to respond quickly
- The fear of falling behind
- The belief that I should be doing more

Just write what you notice:

____

____

____

____

____

____

Exercise 2: The Hidden Stressors List

Not all stress announces itself. Some of it runs quietly in the background. So quietly, in fact, that you stop noticing it. You assume it's just part of life.

This exercise helps you gently uncover what might be draining you without you realizing it. Take your time with this one. You may not see everything right away.

Step 1: Subtle Pressures
Read through the list below and place a check next to anything that feels familiar.

- ☐ I feel guilty when I rest.
- ☐ I replay conversations in my head.
- ☐ I worry about how I'm perceived.
- ☐ I compare myself to others online.
- ☐ I feel behind in life.
- ☐ I feel responsible for other people's emotions.
- ☐ I struggle to say no.
- ☐ I overthink small decisions.
- ☐ I feel like I should be doing more.
- ☐ I rarely feel "caught up."
- ☐ I stay mentally "on" even during downtime.
- ☐ I apologize often, even when it's not necessary.
- ☐ I feel... unseen.
- ☐ Others:

____

____

____

Now... **PAUSE.**

Which three above feel most true for you right now?

1. ____

2. ____

3. ____

Step 2: Background Narratives

Often, hidden stressors are fueled by quiet beliefs. Finish these sentences honestly:

If I slow down, then

____

____.

If I disappoint someone, then

____

____

If I don't respond quickly, then

____

____

If I'm not productive, then

____

____

Notice what your mind fills in.

Gently ask yourself: Are these facts or fears?

☐ Facts

☐ Fears

Step 3: Emotional Carrying Capacity

Sometimes stress isn't about tasks. It's about emotional load. Ask yourself:

☐ Am I pretending to be "fine" when I'm not?

☐ Am I avoiding a conversation I know I need to have?

☐ Am I carrying unresolved resentment?

☐ Am I holding in frustration to keep the peace?

☐ Am I starting to feel like I'm running on empty?

☐ Am I "busy" because I am or because I don't know how to relax?

Write anything that comes up:

____

____

____

____

____

Step 4: What Have You Normalized?

What feels "normal" in your life right now that might actually be draining you? What have you accepted as "just how I am" or "just how life is"?

☐ Checking my phone first thing in the morning

- ☐ Mentally bracing myself for the day that just started
- ☐ Constant background anxiety
- ☐ Working during meals
- ☐ Feeling slightly tense most of the time
- ☐ Doom scrolling at night to "relax"
- ☐ Sleepless nights
- ☐ Others:

____

____

____

Hidden stressors don't shout. They whisper.

They show up as subtle tension, low-level irritability, difficulty resting, or a sense of never fully exhaling.

Hopefully, this exercise has helped you reclaim some form of awareness. Because once something is visible, it's no longer quietly running the show.

Important: There's no need to "fix" anything (unless you want to). The objective here is simply to give yourself a moment to pause and honestly look at how your days are unfolding. The following chapters and exercises will guide you gently, helping you notice patterns, understand what's draining you, and experiment with small shifts at your own pace.

Exercise 3: Where I Feel Most Trapped

Often, feeling like life's "too much" isn't only about busyness. It's about feeling like you don't have a choice over something. This exercise isn't about feeling bad or making drastic decisions. It's about noticing where you might feel constrained. Please take a breath before you begin.

Step 1: Areas of Tightness

In which areas of your life do you feel the most pressure or restriction?

- ☐ Work or career
- ☐ Finances
- ☐ Family dynamics
- ☐ Parenting
- ☐ Relationship
- ☐ Friendships
- ☐ Health
- ☐ Social expectations
- ☐ Time
- ☐ My own thoughts
- ☐ My own habits

Reflect: From the list above, where do you feel the least free?

____

____

____

Step 2: The "I Have To" Statements

Feeling trapped is often tied to rigid internal language. Complete these sentences:

I have to

____

____

I can't

____

____

I should

____

____

I'm supposed to

____

____

Now read your above statements back slowly. Do these feel like absolute truths? Or do they feel like self-imposed pressure?

☐ Absolute truths
☐ Self-imposed pressure

Step 3: The Cost of Staying the Same

Without trying to fix anything, pick a life area (from Step 1) and ask yourself: If nothing changes in this area, how will I feel six months from now? One year from now? Write freely:

____

____

____

____

____

____

Step 4: The Smallest Space of Choice

Even when life feels fixed, there's often a tiny space of choice somewhere.

It may not be in the situation itself. It may be in how you speak to yourself about something, how you respond emotionally, what boundaries you want to experiment with, what conversations you want to avoid, etc.

Reflect: Where, even slightly, do you have more choice than you think?

____

____

____

____

____

Feeling trapped doesn't mean you're weak. It often means you've been carrying too much for too long without space to step back.

Hopefully, this exercise has helped you see which areas of your life deserve a pause, some attention, and maybe down the road, some adjustment.

Chapter 2: Overwhelmed, Angry & Running on Empty

Overwhelm is rarely a single, dramatic event. Instead, it's a cumulative weight; the result of a thousand small stressors that pile up.

In the context of mindfulness, identifying overwhelm isn't just about acknowledging a busy schedule; it's about recognizing the specific physiological and psychological "tells" that signify your system is reaching its capacity.

Most people imagine overwhelm as dramatic: panic attacks, breakdowns, total collapse. In truth, it feels pretty ordinary.

The Physical Echo

When you're overwhelmed, your body often knows before your mind does. It manifests as a low-grade, persistent hum of tension.

You might notice:

The Shallow Breath: Your breathing migrates from the belly to the upper chest, becoming rapid and restricted.

Mini-Mindfulness Exercise

Right now, without changing anything, notice your breath.
Is it deep or shallow?
Is it fast or steady?
Are you breathing into your chest or your belly?

Don't fix it. Just notice.
That simple act of noticing is mindfulness.

The Physical Armor: Your shoulders creep toward your ears, your jaw clenches, or you develop a "tension headache" that feels like a tight band around your temples.

Mini-Mindfulness Exercise

Take five seconds and scan your body.

Are your shoulders lifted?
→ Gently drop your shoulders by one inch.

Is your jaw tight?
→ Rest your tongue at the bottom of your mouth.

Are your hands clenched?
→ Gently open your palms up.

> *No big reset. Just a small release.*
>
> *That's what awareness does. It softens what you didn't realize you were holding.*

Sensory Overload: Suddenly, the humming of the refrigerator feels too loud, the lights feel too bright, and the sensation of your clothes against your skin feels slightly irritating.

Mini-Mindfulness Exercise

Pause for a moment and name:

- *ONE thing you can see*
- *ONE sound you can hear (near or far)*
- *ONE physical sensation you can feel*

You're not escaping the noise.
You're grounding yourself inside it.

The Cognitive Static

Overwhelm doesn't feel like being "too busy." It feels like being paralyzed by choice. This is often referred to as **decision fatigue**.

The Spinning Wheel: You find yourself staring at a grocery store shelf for five minutes, unable to decide between two brands of pasta sauce because the mental energy required to choose feels monumental.

Loss of Perspective: A small mishap, like dropping a piece of toast or a minor typo in an email, feels extremely annoying. That indicates that you no longer have the emotional suspension to absorb the bumps in the road.

The Procrastination Paradox: You have so much to do that you find yourself doing nothing at all, further increasing your anxiety.

Mini-Mindfulness Exercise

Right now, notice your mental speed.

Is your mind racing ahead?
Planning what you'll do next?
Thinking about something you forgot?
Thinking about something you don't want to forget?

Without trying to slow your thoughts down, just label it quietly: ***"Thinking."***

That's it. Just notice.

The Relational Impact

Ever snapped at someone and instantly regretted it? That's because overwhelm rarely stays contained within us; it leaks into our interactions. When you're overwhelmed, your "patience threshold" vanishes. This can look like:

Snap Reactions: You find yourself snapping at a partner, child, or colleague for a minor request. This is usually followed by a wave of guilt, which consumes even more of your limited energy.

Mini-Mindfulness Exercise

Think of the last time you snapped at someone. This isn't about judging or chastising yourself. You're just recalling and observing.

What did you feel in your body right before the words came out? Was there tightness? Heat? Pressure in your chest?

Now imagine that same moment again, but this time, picture a **three-second pause** *before you respond. Count it off if you need to: **3 – 2 – 1**.*

Just three seconds.
That small gap is where mindfulness lives.

Withdrawal: You begin to view social invitations or even simple text messages as "demands" on your time rather than opportunities for connection. You start to isolate because any interaction feels like a potential drain.

The Anger-Exhaustion Cycle

If overwhelm is the *hum* of a system reaching capacity, anger is the spark that happens when that system is finally tapped. And most of the time, your anger isn't really about what happened. It's about how s t r e t c h e d you already were.

When you're well-rested and steady, small inconveniences stay small. You may even laugh at them. But when you're overwhelmed, small inconveniences feel personal. This creates a self-perpetuating loop known as the **Anger-Exhaustion** cycle.

The Energy Cost of Flare-Ups

Anger is an "energy-expensive" emotion. It floods the body with cortisol and adrenaline, demanding a massive surge of metabolic energy. During this state, you'll likely experience:

- **The Spike:** You experience a burst of heat and energy during the outburst.

- **The Crash:** Because your "tank" was already near zero, any sudden energy expenditure like shouting or slamming a door leaves you even more exhausted than before.

- **The Emotional Hangover:** This is a state of lethargy, brain fog, and physical heaviness that follows an episode of high irritability.

The Shame Spiral

The Anger-Exhaustion cycle completes itself through the introduction of *guilt*. After doing something out of anger, you often retreat into self-criticism.

Internalized Exhaustion: You might tell yourself you're a "bad," "unfair," or "mean" parent, partner, friend, or professional.

The Drain of Ruminating: You replay the event in your head, and worrying about the consequences consumes the very last drops of your mental energy.

So, how do you break this Anger-Exhaustion cycle?

Instead of trying to "think" your way out of anger, mindfulness encourages you to address the exhaustion first.

Mini-Mindfulness Exercise: The 60-Second Reset

The next time you feel irritation rising, don't respond immediately. First, quietly ask yourself:

Am I hungry?
Am I lonely?
Am I overstimulated?
Am I tired?

You don't need a deep analysis, just a quick internal scan.

Next, shift your attention to your body.

- *Take one slow breath in.*
- *Then exhale longer than the inhale.*
- *As you exhale, imagine the heat of your emotions lowering by just one degree.*

> - *Do this three times.*
>
> ***Important:*** *You're not trying to eliminate irritation or anger here. You're just creating space around it.*
>
> *If possible, physically move:*
>
> - *Step into another room.*
> - *Wash your hands in cool water.*
> - *Look out a window for ten seconds.*
>
> *Anger feels urgent. But urgency isn't always accuracy.*
>
> *These small interruptions are often enough to stop the anger spiral before it gains momentum.*

Tired But Wired: The Cortisol Loop

You know the feeling. You're exhausted, but the moment you sit or lie down, your mind revs up!

You replay conversations. You mentally prepare for tomorrow. You think about things you forgot to do. Your body feels heavy, but your thoughts just won't slow down. This is the "tired, but wired" state.

When you're stressed, cortisol (the stress hormone) floods your system. In ideal scenarios, you rest or reset, and cortisol leaves your system.

However, we've already covered that modern life means you're bombarded with "little threats" all day long. As such, your body forgets how to return to baseline (relaxation), and you start living in a subtle state of alertness.

You might notice:

- You're easily startled by notifications, people passing by, or even harmless background noise.
- You struggle to relax, even during downtime.
- You feel a strange surge of energy late at night.
- You wake up not fully rested, but tense.
- You experience the *"Where are my keys?"* syndrome, wherein you misplace simple things, forget appointments, or struggle to find common words mid-sentence. *(When you are in the cortisol loop, short-term memory is the first thing to go.)*[4,5]

When you're constantly alert (buzzing), it doesn't mean you have too much energy. It means your body hasn't fully powered down. Over time, this creates a frustrating loop.

And the more this loop repeats, the harder it becomes to tell the difference between busy, stressed, and chronic anxiety. Why? Because *everything* feels slightly urgent.

Mini-Mindfulness Exercise: The Downshift

If you're reading this while feeling slightly tense or mentally busy, try this:

> - *First, sit back just a little (or stand comfortably).*
> - *Breathe in → unclench your jaw.*
> - *Breathe out → let your shoulders drop a fraction.*
> - *Breathe in and then exhale a little longer than you inhaled. Do that three times.*
>
> *Now ask yourself: Right THIS moment, is anything actually wrong? Not tomorrow. Not later. Just **right now**.*
>
> *Next, let your eyes soften and notice the room around you. Realize that you don't need to be on high alert this exact second.*
>
> *This is how mindfulness starts teaching your body that it's allowed to power down.*

Burnout: Running on Empty

In a nutshell, burnout is a state where your energy feels completely depleted. Your motivation has dropped, and you begin to distance yourself from activities that once mattered.

It's not just being tired after a long week. It's waking up tired. It's feeling emotionally drained before the day even begins. It's looking at your responsibilities and thinking, *"I just don't have it in me"* or *"I just can't."*

Burnout is a slow leak.

In recent years, burnout has moved from a quiet personal struggle to a widely recognized issue.[6] Parents feel it. Students feel it. Caregivers feel it. People juggling work and family feel it. Even people who technically "like" their lives feel it.

Burnout has quietly become normal. And that's part of the problem.

When something becomes common, we stop questioning it and start accepting it. But feeling constantly depleted shouldn't be normalized! Burnout isn't something that's just part of "adulthood." It's a signal that something in your life is out of balance and ~~asking~~ begging to be noticed.

Contrary to popular belief, burnout doesn't always look dramatic. Sometimes it looks like:

- Procrastinating on simple tasks
- Snapping at someone (or yourself) over something small
- Doom scrolling endlessly because you can't decide what else to do
- Feeling numb instead of motivated
- Avoiding things you used to care about

Sure, you might still be functioning. You might still be showing up. But inside, you feel flat (or irritable, or disconnected).

So how does mindfulness help?

Mindfulness doesn't magically simplify life. What it does is more subtle and more powerful.

Burnout often comes from operating on autopilot for too long. You keep reacting and keep pushing that you rarely pause long enough to notice how depleted you've become.

Mindfulness interrupts that pattern. It helps you:

- Notice when you're running low *before* you reach empty.
- Recognize irritation *before* it spills over.
- See when you're pushing past your limits *before* your body forces you to stop.
- Become aware of how much you're carrying *before* it starts to feel unbearable.

These might sound small, but they change everything. When you're unaware, you push until you burn out. But when you're aware, you can pause to reset and recharge.

***A quick clarification:** When we talk about burnout in this chapter, we're describing a common pattern of depletion that many people experience when stress goes unmanaged for too long. However, burnout can exist on a spectrum.*

For some, it's mild exhaustion that improves with rest and better boundaries. For others, it can overlap with anxiety, depression, or deeper mental health challenges.

If your fatigue feels extreme, persistent, or accompanied by hopelessness or major changes in functioning, it's important to seek professional support. Mindfulness can be a powerful complement, but it's not a replacement for medical or therapeutic care when that care is needed.

Exercise 4: Burnout—An Honest Inventory

Burnout doesn't usually arrive with a dramatic announcement. It builds gradually. You adapt, you push through, and you normalize feeling stretched... until you can't.

So, this activity is about taking some time to ask yourself: *Where is my energy right now?*

Note: This exercise is an invitation to gently notice what may be taxing you too much right now. If looking at that feels a little overwhelming, that's okay. You can skip this activity for now and come back to it whenever you feel more ready.

Step 1: Energy Snapshot
Without overthinking it, rate your current state from 1–10.
0 = calm and rested, 10 = reaching my limit

Physical energy: ______ / 10
Emotional energy: ______ / 10
Mental clarity: ______ / 10
Motivation: ______ / 10

Take a **pause** here. Take one slow breath.
Don't judge the ratings you gave. Just notice.

Step 2: Signs I Might Be Running Low
Read through and check what feels true recently:

☐ I wake up already tired.
☐ Small tasks feel heavier than they should.

- ☐ I feel detached from things I used to care about.
- ☐ I procrastinate on simple responsibilities.
- ☐ I feel numb more often than I'm motivated.
- ☐ I fantasize about escaping or disappearing for a while.
- ☐ I feel resentful of demands that didn't used to bother me.
- ☐ I rely on caffeine, sugar, or distraction to get through the day.

Which of the above concerns you the most?

Example: Fantasizing about escaping or disappearing for a while. I often imagine being somewhere and just enjoying myself and not worrying about anything.

____

____

____

____

____

Step 3: Energy Expenditure & Restoration

Burnout is about giving more than you restore.

List three things that regularly drain you:

1. _____________________________________

2. _____________________________________

3. _____________________________________

Now list three things that genuinely refill you (not distractions, things that give you real energy restoration):

Example: going to the gym and not having to rush home; meal planning and eating healthily; being "off" and unreachable from work after 5 PM

1. ____

2. ____

3. ____

Step 4: One Small Adjustment

If you can't do or commit to doing your Top 3 energy fillers above, what's one small, realistic adjustment you could make this week that would protect your energy?

☐ Go to bed 30 minutes earlier.
☐ Silence nonessential notifications after 9 pm.
☐ Take a 10-minute walk alone.
☐ Say no to one optional commitment.
☐ Leave one email unanswered until tomorrow.
☐ Others:

____

____

Important: You don't start addressing burnout with willpower. You begin by *noticing*, and then by protecting your energy in small, consistent ways.

Part 2: Calming Your Mind

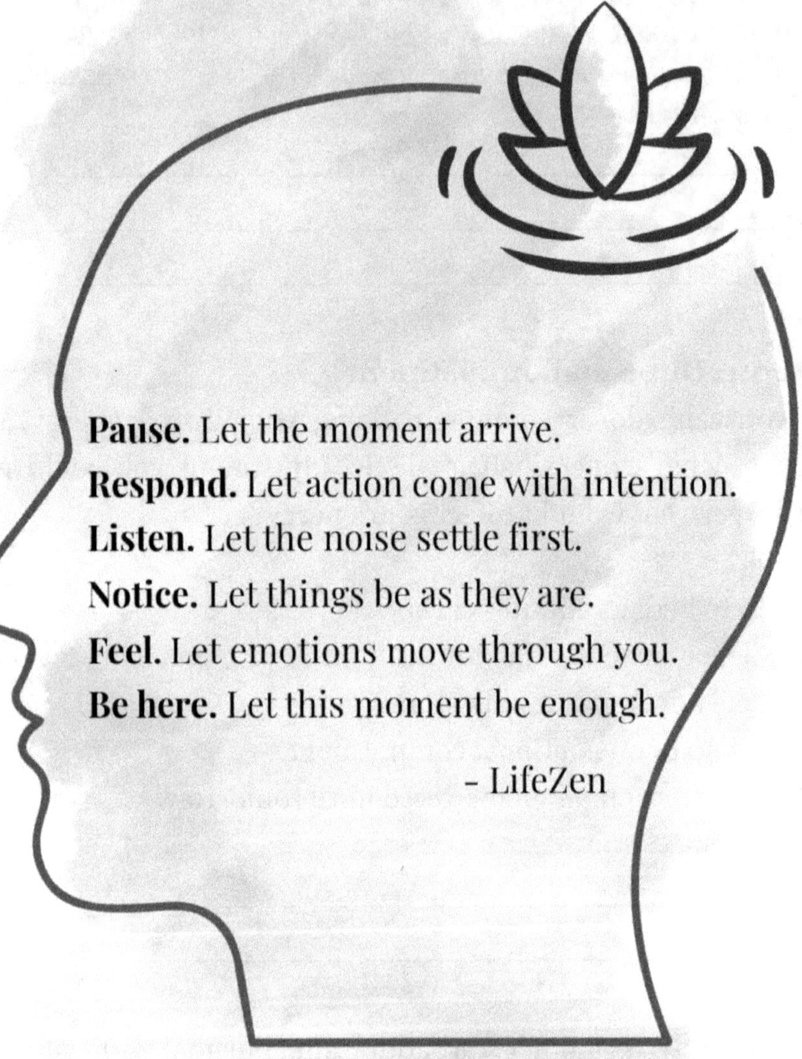

Chapter 3: Mindfulness That Actually Makes Sense (No Fluff!)

Right now, you might be thinking: *"Okay. I get it. The world is loud, scary, and messy. I'm overloaded. I'm stretched thin."* But what exactly is mindfulness supposed to do about that?

Depending on where you're coming from, mindfulness can seem mystical, spiritual, religious, complicated, or only for people who enjoy sitting silently for long periods.

Let's clear something up immediately.

Mindfulness is NOT about becoming calm all the time, or taking a moment to "empty your mind." It's not about pretending everything is okay. And it has nothing to do with time. It's much simpler than that.

Mindfulness is simply this: Paying attention to what is happening, *on purpose*, without immediately trying to change it.

We're so used to rushing every day that what happens is **Trigger→Reaction**. For example, say in the middle of a hectic day, someone drops something, and you just blurt out, *"What now?!"* What do you think the other person would feel? (What would *you* feel if that other person were you?)

Mindfulness is **Trigger** → → → → → **Response**. For example, say in the middle of a hectic day, someone drops something. But this time, you take a breath... you create space... and say... *"What happened? Are you ok?"* What do you think the other person would feel? (What would *you* feel if that other person were you?)

THAT is the power of mindfulness.

For this reason, I also think of mindfulness as a **mental pause**. Many people assume mindfulness requires carving out serious time, like blocking off an hour in an already over packed schedule. In truth, **mindfulness doesn't need a dramatic stop.**

You don't need to shut everything down. You just want to introduce a brief interruption in the automatic flow of rushing, judging, and reacting. It's that brief moment between stimulus (trigger) and response (acting based on impulse).

It's the second where you notice, *"Oh, I'm getting irritated,"* or *"My mind is spiraling,"* or even, *"Hmmm, I'm more tired than I realized."*

That mental pause doesn't remove the situation. It doesn't solve the problem instantly. But it creates space.

And in that space, you get the chance to choose the next step that can make the situation better.

Simply put, **mindfulness gives you the opportunity to think *before* you say or do something that might make a situation worse.**

Instead of reacting, you take a moment to notice what's happening *in your mind*. That small pause gives you the chance to respond thoughtfully instead of impulsively.

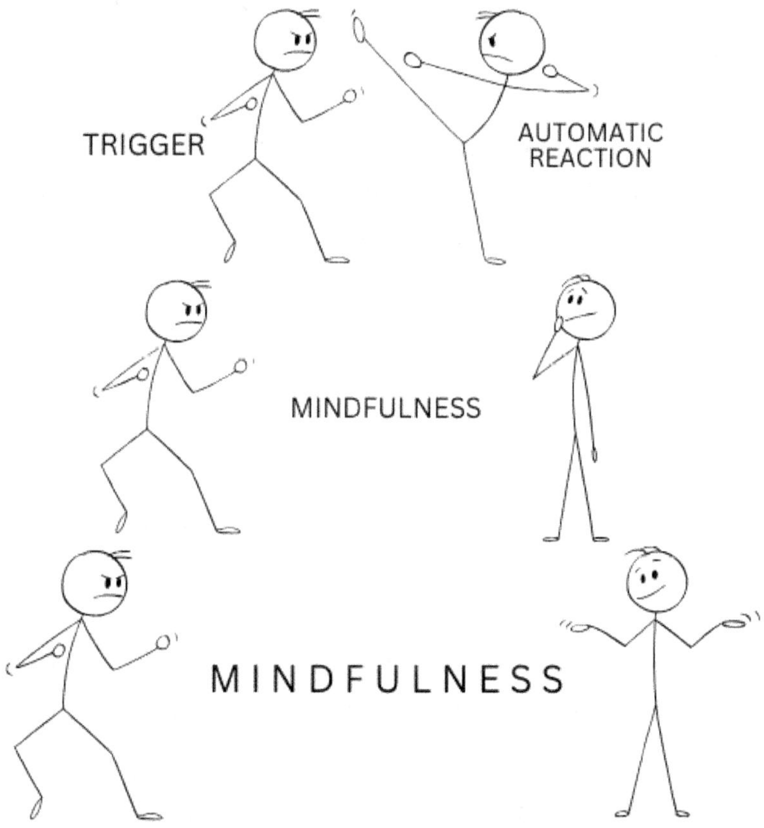

Now, when we say *"before you say or do something that might make a situation worse,"* many people assume this is for other people's benefit, like you don't want to say or do something that might hurt someone's feelings.

And yes, that matters. But the deeper benefit is actually *for you.*

When you react impulsively (e.g., snap at someone, send the angry text, fire off the email, slam the door, etc.), you don't just affect the other person. You affect yourself; your own peace and your own energy. How?

You often end up with regret, guilt, rumination, and more stress than you started with. For example, one reactive moment can turn into hours of replaying the scene in your head.

Mindfulness steps in before that spiral begins, thereby protecting your future self.

So yes, not making a situation worse can benefit others. But just as importantly, it keeps you from adding extra suffering to your own day.

Mindfulness isn't about being nice for the sake of appearances. It's about not creating unnecessary chaos in your own mind.

Mindfulness is also non-judgmental.

When you're overwhelmed, angry, tired, or make a mistake, mindfulness doesn't shame you for it. It doesn't apply labels or make demands. It simply says, *"This is what's here right now."*

And that small shift in thinking changes everything.

Instead of arguing with your feelings, you acknowledge them. Instead of criticizing yourself for having a reaction, you notice the reaction.
Instead of blaming someone, you pause long enough to understand what's really happening inside you.

Think of it this way: You see a leaf drifting down the stream. Mindfulness says, *"There's a leaf drifting down a stream."* No more. No less.

Mindfulness is the doorway to acceptance— and from acceptance, you can gain clarity. And from clarity, things often get better.

On one side of that doorway is resistance: fighting your feelings, blaming yourself, reacting automatically.

On the other side is acceptance: seeing clearly what's happening without adding guilt, shame, or panic.

Acceptance doesn't mean you like what's happening. It means you stop arguing with *what is* (reality) long enough to respond wisely.

And from that place, "better" becomes possible.

You can make better decisions, apply better boundaries, have better conversations, cultivate better relationships, and take better care of your own energy.

Mindfulness doesn't force change. It creates the space where change can happen.

Mindfulness vs. Meditation

Many people confuse mindfulness with meditation. So, here's the clarification:

Mindfulness is a way of relating to experience.
*It's a **quality** of awareness and attention you build.*

Meditation is a formal practice.
*Meditation is something you do. It's an **activity**.*

You can meditate for 60 seconds or 5 minutes in the morning. But you can be mindful while eating, washing dishes, driving, listening to someone, standing in line, etc.

Note: Meditation *is* one of the most effective ways to strengthen mindfulness, and we'll explore that later. But you don't need to start there.

For now, think of mindfulness as a subtle shift in how you move through your day. Start the "noticing."

Notice when your mind drifts.

Notice when your emotion spikes.
Notice when you're rushing.
Notice when you're holding tension.

That's it.

You're simply training yourself to be aware of your experience as it unfolds.

Exercise 5: The 2-Minute Noticing Experiment

You've read about mindfulness. Now you're going to experience it. For 120 seconds, you're going to practice "noticing."

Step 1: Set a Timer

Set a timer for two minutes. Sit comfortably. You can close your eyes or keep them softly open. There's nothing to "achieve" here.

Step 2: Just Notice

For the next two minutes, your only job is to observe.

Notice:
- How you're sitting
- What your body feels like while sitting
- What sounds are present
- What thoughts are passing through
- What emotions (if any) are there

You're not trying to do anything. You're just "watching."

Step 3: Label Gently

If it helps, softly label what you notice.

"Thinking" or "I'm thinking."
"Hearing" or "Hearing something."
"Tightness."
"Planning."
"Irritation."

No long explanations needed. Just simple labels.

Labeling helps create space.

Step 4: When Your Mind Wanders

Even in just 120 seconds, your mind will drift. That's normal. When you notice that you're caught in a thought, gently bring your attention back to observing. Remember, the moment you realize you wandered *is* mindfulness.

Step 5: When the Timer Ends

Before you move on, pause for one breath. Then gently reflect:

What did I notice?
Was my mind busy? Calm? Restless?
Did I judge what was happening?
Did anything shift?

If nothing comes to you, that's okay.

Step 6: What Just Happened?

For two minutes, you practiced observing how it is to be still. Try this once a day for a week. Not to perfect it, but just to become more familiar with your own mind.

Positivity vs. Presence

Another misunderstanding is that mindfulness means thinking only positive thoughts. It doesn't.

If you're overwhelmed, mindfulness doesn't tell you to say: *"This is okay"* or *"Oh, don't be dramatic."* What it does is it invites you to say: *"I notice I feel overwhelmed."*

Positivity is a mindset that seeks out the best in any situation. That's incredibly useful for resilience and motivation, but it has a specific agenda: **it wants things to be better**.

Presence, however, doesn't care if the moment is "good" or "bad." It's simply **the act of being anchored in the now**. If you're eating a delicious meal, you're present with the flavor. If you stub your toe, you're present with the throbbing pain.

When you strive for positivity, you're often in a subtle conflict with reality whenever things go wrong (because you want things to be better). But when you strive for presence, you stop fighting reality.

And that's what mindfulness achieves in the long run: for you to be at peace with *what is*.

Because even though you might be experiencing something difficult or painful, being present often brings a deeper and more stable sense of peace than trying to force yourself into a better mood.

Exercise 6: Seeing the Space Between

Our brains are very quick to label things: Chair. Phone. Coffee mug. Person. However, once a label appears, the brain often stops looking further and returns to its internal chatter. This exercise helps you experience the moment without relying on labels or judgments.

Step 1: Select Two Objects

Wherever you are, choose two objects in your line of sight (e.g., a lamp and a monitor, a coffee mug and a pen, etc.).

Step 2: Look at the Space Between

Don't look at the objects themselves. Instead, shift your attention to the **space** between them. For example, focus on the space between a coffee mug and a pen, or the thin sliver of light between two books.

Step 3: Trace the Space

Using only your eyes, slowly follow the outline of that empty space. Notice where one object ends, and the open space begins. Let your eyes move slowly around the edges of the gap.

Step 4: Observe the Texture of Nothing

Stay with the space for about 30–60 seconds. Ask yourself:

How large is the space?
Does the light change across it?
Does the shape of the gap resemble anything?

There is no correct answer. The goal is simply to observe.

Reflection:

How did this exercise feel?
Did your mind slow down even slightly?
Did you notice details you normally ignore?
Write a few words below:

____

____

____

____

____

____

____

This exercise interrupts the brain's habit of labeling and judging. When you shift attention to something as simple as space, your mind has fewer stories to tell... and what remains is presence.

Why Awareness Brings Relief

Here's something subtle but powerful: the moment you notice you're overwhelmed... you're no longer consumed by it. *(In psychology, this shift is called **cognitive defusion**, the ability to step back and observe your thoughts and feelings instead of being consumed by them or glued to them.)[7]*

When you practice awareness, you create a tiny separation. It's like saying:

I am here. •
The feeling is there. →

And that gap, however small, brings relief. That's not because the stress vanished, but because your brain has "shifted gears." When you name or become aware of what you're feeling, the emotional center of the brain quiets slightly. You move from being inside the storm to observing it. And observation activates the thinking part of your brain, the part that can choose.

Awareness → Relief → Return of Choice

Let me share something I do when my mind starts scattering, and I'm feeling the beginnings of stress.

Sometimes, I get so busy with my writing and everything else that involves being a published author that I sometimes feel my thoughts scattering in the morning. Like I start with "A," which triggers "B," so I quickly hop on that, but then that triggers "C."

Before I know it, my mind is spinning out into a dozen different directions.

When I notice this, I completely STOP what I'm doing. (Sometimes, I literally push my chair away from my desk.) I grab a pen and paper and start writing down everything that's bouncing around in my head. Not in an organized way. Not in a polished way. Just a quick brain dump.

I write down the ideas, the tasks, the worries, the "don't forget this" thoughts, the half-formed plans... all of it. I don't judge it, and I don't prioritize it. I just get it out of my head and onto paper.

Within a few minutes, something shifts.

The spinning slows down, the urgency drops, and what felt chaotic starts to look manageable. Instead of ten competing thoughts pulling at me, I can see them clearly in front of me.

Then I ask myself one simple question: What needs my attention *right now*? I don't need to do everything. I just need to figure out the next step.

That small pause doesn't eliminate my responsibilities. It doesn't magically reduce my workload. But it interrupts the mental avalanche. It turns scattered thinking into deliberate action. And that's the power—and relief—that mental pause does for me.

Exercise 7: Brain Dump

When thoughts stay in your head, they feel bigger and more urgent. When you put them on paper, they become visible, and visibility reduces pressure.

Step 1: Set a Timer (5–10 Minutes)

Choose a short, contained window of time. Five minutes is enough, but choose ten if you feel particularly scattered. Setting a specific time matters because you subconsciously tell yourself you're not doing this all day. You're just creating a pause.

Step 2: Write Everything Down

On a blank sheet of paper (or more), begin writing down **everything** that is currently pulling at your attention.

- Things you need to do
- Things you forgot to do
- Conversations you're replaying
- Worries about tomorrow
- Annoyances
- Deadlines
- Ideas
- Guilt
- "Don't forget this" reminders
- Random mental clutter

DO NOT organize. DO NOT prioritize. DO NOT analyze. DO NOT judge whether something is "important enough." If it's taking up space in your mind, dump it on the page. Keep your pen moving.

Step 3: Notice the Tone of Your Thoughts

After the timer ends, pause. Look at what you wrote. Without changing anything, **simply observe**:

- Are these unfinished tasks?
- Are most of these urgent?
- Are they self-critical?
- Are they emotional reactions?
- Are they future-focused?

Remember, you're just noticing here. This is mindfulness in action.

Step 4: Circle What Actually Needs Action RIGHT NOW or TODAY

Gently shift gears. From the entire list, circle only what truly needs your attention right now or today. Often, you'll find that only a few items qualify for "right now" or "today." That realization alone reduces pressure.

Step 5: Choose ONE Next Step

From the circled items, choose one small next action. Not the whole project, just the next physical step. For example:

- If you circled, "Finish report," write "Open document and review first paragraph."

- If you circled "Reply to brother," write "Send message to check in."

Mindfulness turns vague overwhelm into specific action.

Step 6: Reflect

Before moving on with your day, ask yourself: *How does my mind feel now compared to before I wrote everything down?*

Often, you'll find that the "spinning" slows, the urgency softens, and what felt chaotic becomes contained.

That's the mental pause at work.

Step 7: Optional Practice

If you like, you can repeat this brain dump exercise:

- At the start of the day
- At the end of the week
- On Sunday evening
- Before bed, if your mind is racing
- Whenever you feel scattered

Distraction as the Modern-Day Default

Why is "paying attention on purpose" so difficult? It's because we're used to being constantly distracted.

Most of us wake up and reach for our phones before we're fully awake. Notifications, messages, headlines, reminders... the day hasn't even started yet, but our attention is already divided. And it's not just digital distraction; there's also internal distraction.

You sit down to work and suddenly remember something you forgot yesterday (past) or need to do tomorrow (future). You begin one task, and your mind jumps to another. Even in silence, the mind rarely stays still for long.

This doesn't mean you're incapable of focus. It means that you've gotten used to your attention being easily hijacked.

Further, distraction often feels easier than presence. When something feels uncomfortable, boring, or emotionally charged, the mind looks for an exit. Suddenly, a notification, a new thought, or a quick task is an escape. It's something to shift away from what's happening right now. Because if you stayed in the moment, you might notice something you've been avoiding.

But every time attention is pulled away unconsciously, awareness weakens just a little.

Mindfulness isn't about eliminating all distractions; that's unrealistic. It's about recognizing when attention has drifted and gently bringing it back. That's the practice.

Exercise 8: Distraction Habit Tracker

Distraction isn't a personal failure. It's a pattern. And the first step in changing any pattern is seeing it clearly.

When you begin to notice distraction *as it happens*, something subtle changes. Instead of being completely pulled away, you become aware of the pull. And that moment of awareness is where mindfulness begins.

Step 1: Notice the Moment of Drift

Over the next day or two, pay attention to moments when your focus suddenly shifts away from what you're doing.

For example:
- You open your phone while working.
- You switch tabs or apps repeatedly.
- You keep checking your email "just in case."
- Your mind starts planning or replaying conversations.
- You leave one task unfinished and start another.

Each time you notice your attention drifting, make a quick note.
Example:
Working on a report → checked my phone → started scrolling.

____

____

____

____

____

Step 2: What Triggered the Distraction?

Look at the situations you listed. What seemed to trigger the distraction? Possible triggers include:

- Boredom
- Frustration with a task
- Feeling overwhelmed
- Waiting for something
- A notification or alert
- Habit (checking without thinking)
- Avoiding something difficult

What are your distraction triggers?

____

____

____

____

Step 3: What Did the Distraction Give You?

Distraction usually serves a purpose. Even if it's brief, it often provides relief. Ask yourself: *What did the distraction give me in that moment?*

For example:

- A break from effort
- A quick burst of stimulation
- Escape from discomfort
- Something easier to focus on

Write your observations:

____

____

____

Step 4: Reflect

When does distraction show up most often for me?

____

____

____

____

What emotions or situations tend to trigger it?

____

____

____

____

Are there patterns I didn't notice before?

____

____

____

____

The "Zen Myth" that Holds People Back

It's a common mental image: a person sitting cross-legged, perfectly still, eyes closed, and possessing a mind as empty and silent as a vacuum.

But if that's your benchmark for mindfulness, you're setting yourself up for a lot of unnecessary frustration. Let's clear this up.

Myth 1: The "Empty Mind" Fallacy

Many people quit mindfulness because they "can't stop thinking." They assume the goal is to eliminate every thought until the brain becomes blank.

The Reality: The brain is a thought-generating organ, much like the heart is a blood-pumping organ. Expecting the brain to stop thinking is like asking your lungs to stop breathing.

The Realization: Mindfulness isn't about stopping thoughts; it's about changing your relationship to them. You transition from being "caught in the storm" to "watching the storm."

Myth 2: You Must Be "Chill" 24/7

This myth suggests that mindful people are emotionless statues who never get angry, stressed, or impatient.

The Reality: Mindfulness makes you *more* aware of your emotions, not less. You'll still feel the spike of adrenaline when someone cuts you off in traffic.

The Realization: Instead of a blind reaction, you gain a "micro-gap" of awareness with mindfulness. You feel the anger, acknowledge it (*Grrrr, there's a tight feeling in my chest right now*), and then choose how to respond in a way that makes the situation better for you.

Myth 3: Mindfulness Is Escaping Reality

Some believe mindfulness means zoning out or retreating into a blissful bubble.

The Reality: Mindfulness is the opposite. It's zoning in. It's being fully present with what's happening, even when it's uncomfortable, boring, or painful.

The Realization: Mindful people don't escape reality; they accept it as it is. When you see things as they are, and not as you wish they were, you reduce unnecessary mental friction.

Mindfulness isn't about achieving some heightened or mystical state of awareness. It's much simpler than that.

It's about slowing down just enough to notice what is already happening. Your thoughts. Your emotions. Your reactions. Just simply noticing the moment you're in.

Exercise 9: Resistance to Slowing Down

Mindfulness is noticing what is already happening. But when people first try to slow down, something interesting often happens: they feel restless.

Suddenly, the urge appears to check your phone, open another tab, start a new task, or fill the silence with something... anything. This exercise helps you notice that urge.

Step 1: List Three Main Activities from Your Day

Think about your day so far (or yesterday). Write down three big activities you spent time on. Examples might include work, errands, cooking dinner, meetings, commuting, or taking care of family responsibilities.

1. ____

2. ____

3. ____

Step 2: Look at the Spaces Between

Now think about the moments *between* those activities. For example:

- The walk from one room to another
- Waiting for something to load
- Standing in line
- Sitting in the car
- The minutes before a meeting starts

Write down a few of those in-between moments.

Step 3: Notice What Filled Those Moments

When those small gaps appeared, what did you do? Did you:

- ☐ Reach for your phone
- ☐ Check messages or email
- ☐ Turn on music or a podcast
- ☐ Start thinking about the next task
- ☐ Replay conversations in your mind
- ☐ Others:

Step 4: Reflect

Now ask yourself: *Why did I feel the need to "fill" those moments? Why was I not able to allow those small moments to simply exist?*

Write your observations:

____

____

____

Sometimes the space between activities feels uncomfortable because it allows your thoughts (the deep, real, and honest kind) to surface. And sometimes, well, you fill the in-between moments because that's what you're used to doing.

Mindfulness invites you to notice those small gaps instead of hurrying past them. Remember, you don't have to rush through life. Slowing down, even briefly, is something you can choose.

Chapter 4: How to Relax When You Don't Know How

How do I make myself relax?
Why can't I calm down?
Why do I feel wired even when nothing's happening?
Why does trying to relax sometimes make me even tenser?!

Now that you know what mindfulness truly is (and isn't), **how do you try to relax in today's world?** That may seem like a simple question, but it's not at all.

You lie down.
You close your eyes.
You put your phone away.
You tell yourself, *"Okay. Now, I'm going to relax."*
And then... nothing happens.
Or worse, your thoughts get louder. So what's going on?

It's because **relaxation isn't a decision.**

When you "decide" to relax, your mind may interpret it as pressure to do (or be) something. So, it's not something you achieve by force. In fact, the more you *try*, the more tension you might create.

So, here's what you need to understand: **Relaxation is a shift, not a switch.**

NOT: How do I make myself relax?

BUT: How do I reduce the pressure that's keeping me tense?

The following are **REAL-LIFE scenarios** and what you can do to reduce that building pressure (and achieve relaxation).

Scenario: The Tense Family Gathering

The pressure:	You're bracing for awkward comments, old conflicts, or passive-aggressive remarks.
What's building the tension:	Anticipating every possible trigger.
Reduce the pressure:	Drop the expectation that things have to go well. Tell yourself: "I don't need to manage everyone." When triggered, deliberately slow your breathing before responding. If things feel too much, excuse yourself for a short reset if needed.
Relaxation goal:	Relaxation here means lowering the need to control the room. Relaxation here is to stop "bracing for impact" because anticipation often creates more stress than the moment itself.

Scenario: The Boring Conversation

The pressure:	You feel trapped. You want out, but you're trying to be polite.
What's building the tension:	Forcing enthusiasm.
Reduce the pressure:	Stop trying to "look interested." Relax your jaw. Listen for one detail instead of the whole story.
Relaxation goal:	Relaxation here means dropping the performance.

Scenario: The "I Can't Sleep" Situation

The pressure:	Your mind starts solving tomorrow's problems.
What's building the tension:	Trying to force sleep.
Reduce the pressure:	Stop aiming for sleep. Aim for rest. Tell yourself: "Just lying here is enough." Slow your exhales; make them slightly longer than your inhales.
Relaxation goal:	Relaxation here means removing the goal (sleeping).

Scenario: The Inbox Overload Conundrum

The pressure:	Unread emails. Notifications. The need to

	rush so you don't fall "behind."
What's building the tension:	Believing you must clear everything immediately.
Reduce the pressure:	Choose one message. Just one. Lower the bar from "finish" to "start."
Relaxation goal:	Relaxation here means narrowing your focus.

Scenario: The Argument is Escalating Dilemma

The pressure:	Your chest tightens. Rebuttal words are forming fast.
What's building the tension:	Needing to win or prove your point.
Reduce the pressure:	Take a 3-5 second mental pause. Say, "Let me think about that." Notice the tightness in your chest instead of firing back.
Relaxation goal:	Relaxation here means choosing space over speed, mindful breaths over words.

Scenario: The Waiting Game

The pressure:	The act of waiting itself (for test results, a reply, a decision, etc.).
What's building the tension:	Trying to predict outcomes.

Reduce the pressure:	Shift from "What will happen?" to "What is happening right now?" Notice where your hands are. Notice your feet on the ground. Look around and notice three neutral things (e.g., a cup, a painting, a stuffed toy).
Relaxation goal:	Relaxation here means stepping out of future projection.
Scenario: The Social Media Spiral	
The pressure:	Scrolling. Comparing. Reacting.
What's building the tension:	Unconscious consumption.
Reduce the pressure:	Put the phone down for 60 seconds. Put your hands together and feel the warmth you're self-generating. Take one slow breath. Ask, "Is what I'm consuming helping me in any way?"
Relaxation goal:	Relaxation here means interrupting momentum.
Scenario: The Overloaded To-Do List	
The pressure:	Too many tasks. Not enough time.

What's building the tension:	Thinking about all of it at once.
Reduce the pressure:	Write down one, next physical action. Not the whole project. Just the next step.
Relaxation goal:	Relaxation here means shrinking the frame.

Scenario: The "Silent Room After Conflict" Space

The pressure:	You're replaying what was said.
What's building the tension:	Mentally rewriting the conversation.
Reduce the pressure:	Notice the replay. Label it: "Rehearsing." "Rewriting." Return attention to your breath or surroundings.
The pressure:	Relaxation here means disengaging from mental loops.

Scenario: The "I Should Be Doing..." Moment

The pressure:	You sit down to rest, but guilt creeps in.
What's building the tension:	Believing rest must be earned.
Reduce the pressure:	Tell yourself: "Rest is part of productivity."

	Set a 10-minute timer. Commit to resting fully for that window, even if that just means closing your eyes.
Relaxation goal:	Relaxation here means removing self-judgment.
Scenario: The "I Don't Know What to Do with Myself" Condition	
The pressure:	There's nothing urgent happening... and that feels uncomfortable.
What's building the tension:	The belief that you must always be engaged, productive, entertained, or improving.
Reduce the pressure:	Do nothing on purpose for 2 minutes. No phone. No task. No fixing. Just sit and notice the urge to move. Say to yourself: "There doesn't have to be something happening right now."
Relaxation goal:	Relaxation here means allowing space without rushing to fill it.
Scenario: The Waiting in Line Irritation	
The pressure:	You're stuck. Delayed. Not in control.
What's building the tension:	The belief that your time is being wasted.

Reduce the pressure:	Unclench your jaw. Drop your shoulders. Treat the line as an opportunity to pause instead of thinking it is stealing time from you.
Relaxation goal:	Relaxation here means surrendering micro-control.

Scenario: The "Perfection Pressure" Problem

The pressure:	You're about to send an email, submit work, post something... but you keep on tweaking.
What's building the tension:	Needing things to be flawless.
Reduce the pressure:	Lower the bar from "perfect" to "clear." Send/post at 90%.
Relaxation goal:	Relaxation here means releasing perfection.

Scenario: The "What Am I Missing?" (FOMO) Moment

The pressure:	You see others doing something. Posting something. Achieving something. Gathering somewhere.
What's building the tension:	Comparison and the fear of being left behind.

Reduce the pressure:	Pause and name it: "This is FOMO." Not truth. Not urgency. Just fear of missing out. Remind yourself: "Not doing something doesn't mean I'm falling behind."
Relaxation goal:	Relaxation here means letting go of the need to keep up with everything.

The big takeaway: Did you notice a pattern in the above scenarios? **Relaxation isn't about escaping life. It's about lowering unnecessary internal pressure within it.**

And mindfulness is what makes that possible.
You notice the pressure. You reduce the pressure.

That's how you achieve relief. That's how rest begins to happen.

Exercise 10: Internal Pressure Audit

Much of the tension we carry comes from internal expectations; i.e., the belief that we should respond faster, do more, handle everything well, keep everyone happy, etc.

This exercise helps you identify where that pressure might be coming from and how to reduce it, so that you can finally relax.

Step 1: Identify One Area That Feels Pressured

Think about a situation in your life where you often feel tense, rushed, or overwhelmed.

☐ Work
☐ Family responsibilities
☐ Social situations
☐ Expectations I place on myself
☐ Others:

____

____

____

Step 2: Identify the Expectation

Ask yourself: *What expectation am I placing on myself in this situation?*

☐ I should handle everything perfectly.
☐ I don't want to be blamed.
☐ I should respond immediately.
☐ I don't want to look "less."

☐ I shouldn't disappoint anyone.

☐ I don't want to seem incapable.

☐ Others:

____

____

____

Step 3: Question the Pressure

Look at the expectations you identified. Ask yourself:

Is this expectation realistic all the time?

____

____

____

What might happen if I lowered this pressure just a little?

____

____

____

Step 4: Define a More Realistic, Flexible Standard

Instead of aiming for perfection, define a more realistic, human, or flexible approach. Examples:

I will respond when I'm ready.

Doing my best today is enough.

Not every situation requires a perfect response.

Not every person has a right to my time and mental space.

Write a healthier standard you can remind yourself of:

____

____

____

____

____

Chapter 5: Learning to Pause

In the previous chapter, you learned how to apply mindfulness *in the moment* and how to lower pressure while you're in the middle of a tense situation.

This chapter builds on that skill by teaching you how to *extend* that moment of mindfulness deliberately. And the reason this matters is simple: most of your stress doesn't come from the situation itself, but from how quickly you react to it.

In everyday life, reactions happen fast. Someone says something irritating, and you say or do something before you've fully processed it. An email arrives, and you immediately assume the worst, or feel the need to answer NOW. A thought pops into your mind, and within seconds, you're building a story around it.

None of this makes you flawed. It makes you human. Your mind is designed to move quickly. But speed isn't always helpful.

As mentioned, mindfulness helps you to pause, even briefly, to interrupt that automatic chain reaction. You create a small space between *what happened* and *what happens next.*

That space may only last a few seconds, but it changes everything. It gives awareness time to catch up with the impulse.

Learning to pause doesn't mean slowing your entire life down or becoming passive. It **means strengthening your ability**

to delay reaction just long enough to decide how you actually want to respond.

A pause is the difference between:

- Sending a text immediately and rereading it once before you do.
- Snapping at someone and taking one breath before speaking.
- Blaming someone for a situation and taking a moment to ask yourself what you may have done to contribute to it.

You already know that awareness brings relief. Here, you'll practice stretching that awareness just a little longer. Because the longer you can stay present *before* reacting, the more intentional your actions become.

So, how do you cultivate the skill of learning to pause? Through Breathwork, Meditation, and taking Deliberate Pauses.

Breathwork That Actually Calms You

Why start here? Because your breath is always with you. It doesn't require silence, special posture, extra time, a quiet room, or any fancy equipment. You can use it in the middle of a conversation, while standing in line, sitting in traffic, or reading an email that just triggered you.

More importantly, **your breath reflects your state of mind.** When you're anxious, it becomes shallow and quick. When you're tense, you may hold it without realizing it. When you're calm, it naturally slows.

The **breath also sits at the intersection of automatic and intentional**. It happens on its own, but you can also guide it. That makes your own breathing the perfect bridge into mindfulness.

When you bring your attention to your breath, even for a few seconds, you're doing two things at once. First, you're interrupting whatever mental momentum is building. Second, you're anchoring your attention to something concrete and present.

The exercises that follow are progressive. Start with the simplest one. Let it become familiar, and then extend the pause gradually. Consistency matters more than intensity.

Important: You're not trying to master breathing. You're practicing pausing using the power of your own breath.

Exercise 11: One Conscious Breath

This is the simplest and shortest possible pause you can take.

1. Wherever you are, take one slow breath in through your nose.
2. Next, exhale gently through your mouth.
3. As you exhale, imagine releasing just 5% of tension. Not all of it. Just a little.

That's it! You're not trying to relax fully. You're interrupting "autopilot."

Practice this throughout the day, like before answering a question, before getting into your car, before sending a message, before standing up from your desk, before stepping out of the shower, and so on.

One conscious breath is enough to create space.

Exercise 12: 10-Breath Reset

Let's extend the pause slightly with this practice.

1. Sit or stand comfortably.
2. Close your eyes if that feels safe.
3. Begin counting your breaths from one to ten. For example:
    Inhale → exhale → 1
    Inhale → exhale → 2
4. Continue until you reach ten.

In all likelihood, somewhere along the way, you'll get lost, distracted, and forget your counting before you reach "Ten." Whenever that happens, start over with "One."

If you find yourself at, say, "8" without realizing how you got there, then you're still not anchored to the present moment. In this case, start over with "One."

The goal of this exercise isn't perfect focus. The goal is *to return*.

Exercise 13: Box Breathing

This breath practice introduces *structure*. You're not forcing calm here. You're just giving your mind something steady to follow.

1. Inhale for four counts.
2. Hold for four counts.
3. Exhale for four counts.
4. Hold for four counts.
5. Repeat this cycle (steps 1-4) five times.

If four counts feel too long, reduce it to three. If it feels too easy, extend to five.

In this exercise, the symmetry creates rhythm, and rhythm creates steadiness.

Exercise 14: Extended Exhales

This technique gently reduces internal urgency.

1. Inhale through your nose for a count of four.

1	2	3	4

2. Exhale slowly for a count of six or seven.

1	2	3	4	5	6	7

The longer exhale signals your system to soften. Continue for two to three minutes.

Optional: If it helps, tap a finger on the squares above as you count. This can make it easier to keep a steady breathing rhythm.

If counting feels stressful, simply focus on making the exhale slightly longer than the inhale. That's enough.

Exercise 15: The 5-Minute Anchor

This exercise is the most sustained pause in this section.

1. Set a timer for five minutes.
2. Sit upright or find a place where you can lie down comfortably.
3. Bring your full attention to the sensation of breathing.

   As you inhale, feel the air entering your nose, notice the rise of your chest, and the subtle movement of your abdomen. Imagine breathing in good vibes.

   As you exhale, slightly open your mouth and feel the air slowly flow through. Notice your abdomen deflating and your chest gently falling. Imagine breathing out stress.

4. When your mind wanders, gently notice where it went. Don't analyze or judge the thought. Resist the urge to "follow" the thought as well. Just notice and then gently return to the breath.

At the start, five minutes may feel longer than expected. That's okay; that's part of the training. You're strengthening your ability to remain present before reacting.

Meditation Made Simple & Realistic

Meditation is an excellent way to practice mindfulness. Why? Because it gives you a controlled environment in which to train your attention.

In everyday life, things happen quickly. Conversations happen one after the other. Emails arrive unexpectedly. Thoughts trigger emotions before you've even noticed them. It can be difficult to practice awareness when everything is happening at once.

But when you choose to sit quietly for a few minutes and focus on something simple like your breath, a sound, or even the flow of your thoughts, you remove most of the external noise. That makes it easier to see what your mind is doing.

And what you'll notice is that your mind wanders—a lot.
Now, the "wandering" itself isn't the problem. Usually, the issue is *where* you let it take you.

For example, follow a thought, and you may never finish the task right in front of you. Follow another, and you may start building a story about something that may not even happen. Before you know it, your mind is spiraling over something that began as a single passing idea.

Meditation is great because it helps you develop the skill of "returning."

Each time you notice your attention drift, and you gently bring it back to the present, you're strengthening the very skill that allows you to pause in daily life.

Note that the goal isn't to eliminate thoughts, but to become more familiar with them without feeling the need to react immediately. Over time, that familiarity creates steadiness.

The following exercises are simple meditation practices designed to help you extend your pause for a little longer. Start with what feels right for you at the moment... but start.

Important: You're not trying to become perfectly calm or thought-free. You're practicing noticing *and* returning.

Exercise 16: Sound Meditation

Sound is always present. You don't have to create it or control it. You simply listen, making it a great medium on which to rest your attention.

1. Set a timer for 3–5 minutes. Sit comfortably. You may close your eyes or soften your gaze.

2. Bring your attention to the sounds around you. Notice distant sounds, nearby sounds, and subtle background noises. You might hear a fan, traffic, voices, footsteps, birds, or the hum of electronics. Simply listen.

    Important: Try not to *search* for sounds. Let them appear and disappear naturally. A sound arises, notice it, then let it fade. And then let the next sound arrive on its own.

3. When your mind wanders, just notice it or label it ("Wandering" or "Drifting") and then gently return your attention to listening.

    Pro Tip: Try not to analyze or assess where the sound is coming from, or build a story around it. For example, if you hear a car pulling into a nearby driveway, try not to think "the neighbor is home," just think "car."

Exercise 17: Thought Watching

This meditation helps you observe thoughts instead of getting carried away by them.

1. Set a timer for 3–5 minutes. Sit comfortably and bring your attention to your breathing for a few moments.

2. Next, shift your attention to the thoughts moving through your mind. Don't try to stop them. Just notice their presence, and then let them pass.

3. If it helps, quietly label what you notice. For example: "thinking," "planning," "remembering," "replaying," "ruminating," "worrying," etc.

   The label helps you recognize the thought without getting pulled into it.

4. Imagine your thoughts like clouds passing across the sky. And just like watching clouds, you're not trying to hold on to them or chasing after them, you're simply watching them move.

Exercise 18: The Single-Object Focus

This exercise strengthens your ability to keep attention on ONE thing at a time.

1. Set a timer for two minutes and then look at the image below. Give it your full attention. What do you notice? Write down all your observations.

Important: Observe the image **non-judgmentally**. Don't analyze it or form an opinion about it. **Simply notice what is there.**

For example, instead of thinking "I like/don't like this shape," stick to simple and neutral observations such as "serrated leaves," "pointy," etc.

2. When the two minutes are up, select a simple object in front of you, like a plant, pen, coffee mug, book, etc. This time, set your timer for 5 minutes.

3. As before, write down all your observations about the object you chose **non-judgmentally**.

4. When your mind drifts, just notice it and then bring your attention back to the object. Remember, each *return* strengthens your ability to stay present.

Exercise 19: Open Awareness

This meditation expands your awareness beyond a single focus. Instead of concentrating on one thing, you allow your attention to notice whatever arises.

1. Set a timer for 5-7 minutes. Sit comfortably and allow your breathing to settle naturally.

2. Notice whatever appears; nothing is excluded. Allow your awareness to include:

   - sounds
   - physical sensations
   - thoughts
   - emotions
   - the movement of your breath

3. When something appears in your awareness, notice it briefly, and then allow your attention to move naturally to the next thing. Try not to "hold on" to anything.

4. If you become caught in a thought, simply notice that and widen your awareness again.

Meditation for People Who Hate Sitting Still

If the thought of setting a timer and sitting still makes you uncomfortable or disinclined to try meditation, you're not alone.

Some people feel restless when sitting quietly, while others simply think better while moving. That doesn't mean meditation isn't for you.

Meditation isn't about sitting still. It's about paying attention, and that attention can happen while walking, washing dishes, stretching, or even making coffee.

The following are great alternatives to sitting meditations.

Exercise 20: Walking Meditation

Walking meditation is exactly what it sounds like: walking while paying full attention to the act of walking. You're not trying to get somewhere quickly here. The goal is to notice the movements of your body as you walk.

Step 1: Choose a Short Path

Find a place where you can walk slowly and safely for a few minutes. Examples: hallway, quiet sidewalk, your living room, a garden path, a nearby park, etc.

You don't need a large space. Even a few steps back and forth works.

Step 2: Slow Down

Start walking *slower* than your normal pace. Remember, this isn't about getting a workout in; it's observation. Let your arms hang naturally and keep your posture relaxed.

Step 3: Notice Each Step

Bring your full attention to the physical sensation of walking. Notice your foot lifting, a leg moving forward, your foot touching the ground, and the weight shifting in your body. Really feel each step as it happens.

Step 4: Let Your Mind Wander (and Return)

Your mind will wander. You may start thinking about your day, a conversation, or something you need to do later.

When you notice this, gently bring your attention back to your step: lift, move, land. Each step becomes your anchor to "now."

Step 5: Continue for 5 Minutes

Walk slowly for a few minutes, paying attention to the rhythm of your movement. If you reach the end of your path, simply turn around and continue. There is no destination; the walk itself is the practice.

Pro Tip: On your next walking meditation, you can gently widen your awareness to extend to the environment around you. You might observe the feeling of the air on your skin, distant and nearby sounds, the colors or shapes around you, light and shadow as you move, and so on.

Exercise 21: Stretching Meditation

Stretching meditation combines slow movement with breathing and attention. As your body moves, your mind has something concrete to follow. That can be especially helpful if sitting quietly makes you feel restless or distracted.

Step 1: Sit Comfortably

Sit in a chair with your feet flat on the floor and your back upright but relaxed. Rest your hands on your lap for a moment and take one slow breath.

Step 2: Inhale - Slowly Raise Your Arms

As you breathe in, slowly raise your arms above your head. Move gently and notice what your body is doing. Pay attention to:

- the upward sweep of your arms
- the stretch in your shoulders
- the rise of your chest as you inhale

Go nice and slow; there's no need to rush. (**Optional:** If it feels comfortable for you, tilt your head back and look up as you raise your arms.)

Step 3: Exhale - Gently Lower Your Arms

As you breathe out, slowly lower your arms back down to your sides. Notice:

- the release in your shoulders
- the feeling of your arms moving downward
- the natural drop of your chest as you exhale

If you lifted your gaze upward, slowly bring your head back down to neutral.

Step 4: Repeat the Movement

Continue raising your arms as you inhale and lowering them as you exhale. Move slowly and smoothly.

Repeat the movement **5–10 times**, keeping your attention on the sensation of stretching and breathing.

Step 5: Notice the Sensations

As you stretch, observe what your body feels like. You may notice:

- tightness in certain muscles
- warmth or relaxation
- the rhythm between breath and movement

Variation:

- Try this activity standing up.
- As you inhale, open your hands wide, spreading your fingers.
- While your arms are raised, gently sway them left to right as you exhale and notice how the movement feels for you.

Exercise 22: Waiting Meditation

Waiting is something we all experience every day.

Waiting in line.
Waiting for a page to load.
Waiting for someone to reply to a message.
Waiting at a red light.

Most of the time, we treat waiting as "wasted time." Our immediate reaction is to reach for our phone, check messages, or look for something to occupy the moment. This exercise invites you to treat waiting differently.

Instead of filling the space, use it as an opportunity to practice mindfulness. Sometimes, mindfulness simply requires using the moments that already exist.

Step 1: Notice the Waiting Moment

The next time you find yourself waiting for something, pause for a moment before reaching for your phone or distracting yourself. Simply acknowledge: "I'm waiting."

Step 2: Bring Your Attention to the Present

While you wait, gently bring your awareness to what is happening inside you. You might notice:

- your breathing
- the feeling of your feet on the ground
- how you're sitting or standing
- what your hands are doing

Next, slowly expand your awareness to what's happening around you. You may notice:

- the person before or after you
- background music that you realize is always playing, but you have somehow "tuned out"
- your immediate surroundings (**Tip**: Do The Single-Object Focus practice.)

Step 3: Watch the Urge to Fill the Space

As you wait, you may feel the urge to do something. Maybe you want to check your phone, look at the time again, or start thinking about the next thing you need to do.

Instead of acting on the urge immediately, just notice it. Recognize the impulse and let it pass.

Step 4: Stay for a Few More Moments

Remain present for at least two minutes, simply observing what is happening around you. Let the waiting be part of the practice.

Using Deliberate Pauses in Daily Life

Breathwork helps you interrupt a stressful moment. Meditation helps you train your attention. Deliberate pauses are where you apply both skills in everyday life.

A deliberate pause is exactly what it sounds like: a small, intentional break between *before and after* or *then and now.*

The pause itself is small, but its effect can be powerful. It gives your awareness time:

(1) **To catch up between trigger and reaction.** For example, if someone raises their voice at you, your impulse might be to raise your voice back.

In this situation, a deliberate pause gives you a moment to notice what's happening inside you. You might notice a rush of anger or tension in your body. This space gives self-awareness, and in turn, you may think, *"Okay, raising my voice back will probably only escalate things. Let me answer calmly instead."*

(2) **To let go of whatever you were holding onto before stepping into what comes next.** For example, suppose you're feeling stressed because you got stuck in traffic on the way home. When you walk through the door, that stress often walks in with you.

In this example, a deliberate pause before entering your home gives you a moment to *reset*. You can take a breath, acknowledge the frustration, and release some of that tension so it doesn't spill into the next part of your day.

The exercises that follow will help you practice inserting these intentional pauses throughout your day. Mind you, the goal isn't to slow your life down dramatically. It's to strengthen your ability to notice what is happening before you act.

Exercise 23: The Question Pause

Sometimes, the fastest way to interrupt an impulsive reaction is to ask yourself a simple question.

A question creates a moment of reflection.[8] Instead of reacting immediately, your mind shifts from impulse to curiosity. This small shift can slow down the mental momentum that often drives stress and conflict.

Step 1: Notice the Trigger

Think of a moment when you feel the urge to react quickly. For example:

- reading a frustrating email
- hearing a critical comment
- feeling pressure to respond immediately
- noticing irritation rising
- when a specific person says something about a specific topic

When you feel that urge, pause for a moment.

Step 2: Ask a Simple Question

Instead of reacting right away, ask yourself **one** of these questions:

- What happened?
  Example: A colleague sent an email asking about something we already discussed last week.
- What are you thinking or feeling? Label it.
  Example: I'm feeling frustrated.
- What would you normally say or do in this situation?
  Example: I would most likely hit "Reply" right away and send a terse (maybe even sarcastic) email.
- What do you think will be the result of saying or doing what you would normally do?
  Example: I guess it might cause some tension between us.
- What response would make this situation better?
  Example: This question doesn't need an immediate answer, so I'll put off replying till I'm less agitated. And then I would reply something like, "As discussed last week..." and then keep things professional.
- Is this person voicing a fact or an opinion? *(If it's a fact, respond to the information. If it's an opinion, recognize that it's simply their perspective.)*

Note: You don't need a perfect answer to these questions. The goal is simply to *interrupt* the automatic reaction.

Step 3: Allow the Pause

Take one slow breath while considering the questions. Often, you'll find that the intensity of a moment softens slightly when you deliberately give yourself time.

Exercise 24: The Delay Tactic

Many reactions feel urgent. A message arrives, and you feel the need to respond immediately. A thought appears, and you feel compelled to act on it. But **urgency is often an illusion**.

The Delay Tactic helps you practice creating space before responding. This mindfulness practice achieves two things: (1) It gives you time to process, and (2) it helps you break the habit of feeling like every message, comment, or situation requires an immediate reply.

Step 1: Choose a Small Delay

The next time you feel the urge to respond immediately to something or someone, delay your reaction slightly.

Try waiting for 10 seconds, after taking one slow breath, or one full minute. The delay doesn't need to be long. Even a short pause can break the automatic chain reaction.

Pro Tip: With consistent practice, you can gradually extend the delay time, giving yourself more space to think before reacting.

Step 2: Observe What Happens

During the delay, notice what your mind is doing. You may observe:

- strong emotions fading slightly
- new thoughts appearing
- a different perspective emerging

The delay allows your awareness to catch up with your impulse.

Step 3: Choose Your Response
After the delay, decide what action actually makes sense, or might make the situation better. You may still respond, or you may realize that no response is needed at all.

The important thing is that the choice is now intentional.

Exercise 25: Transition Pauses
Your day is filled with transitions. You move from one room to another, from one task to the next, from one conversation to a new one.

Often, we carry the emotional residue from one moment directly into the next, and that's not always helpful. A *transition pause* allows you to reset before moving forward.

Step 1: Select a Transition Point
Choose a natural transition point during your day. For example:

- walking through a doorway
- finishing one task before starting another
- entering your home after work
- opening a new email or message
- entering a room before a meeting

Step 2: Take One Conscious Breath

Before continuing, pause briefly. Take one slow breath, and as you inhale, notice your body. As you exhale, allow the previous moment to settle.

Step 3: Reset Your Attention

Ask yourself: *What am I bringing with me into this next moment?*

If you notice any tension, irritation, or stress whatsoever, allow it to soften before continuing. You're not erasing the previous moment. You're simply choosing *not* to carry it forward unnecessarily.

What transition point(s) have you chosen? When during your day could a small transition pause help you reset?

Example: I work from home, so I chose my home office doorway. I think a transition pause just before I walk out of it will help me mentally close the workday and shift into home mode.

____

____

____

____

____

____

____

____

Chapter 6: Clearing Mental Clutter & Constant Noise

Mindfulness starts by taking a moment to pause. However, when the mind is overloaded, you may encounter a flood of reminders, worries, unfinished tasks, and random thoughts instead of calm awareness.

This is mental clutter.

Your mind may be trying to remember things you need to do, replay conversations, track unfinished projects, anticipate future problems, and process information all at the same time. Each of these thoughts pulls on your attention, making it harder to pause and be present.

Mindfulness works best when attention has room to breathe. So, this chapter focuses on clearing some of that mental noise.

The goal isn't to eliminate thinking; it's to reduce the constant mental load that keeps your attention scattered.

By unloading some of what your mind is carrying, you create space for awareness. And once that space exists, mindfulness becomes much easier to practice.

Mental Decluttering (Where to Start)

Imagine opening your internet browser and seeing twenty or thirty tabs open at once.

Each tab represents something unfinished. Something you meant to read, check, respond to, or deal with later. Even if you are only working in one tab, the others still sit there quietly pulling on your attention.

Your mind works in a very similar way.

Unfinished tasks, unresolved decisions, unanswered messages, and lingering worries all become "open tabs" in the background of your thinking. You may not be actively focusing on them, but they're there, occupying mental space.

Mindfulness does not mean ignoring these tabs. Instead, it helps you notice them so they can be handled more deliberately.

The following exercises help you unload some of that mental clutter and close a few of the tabs your mind has been holding open.

Exercise 26: Closing Mental Browser Tabs

Just like a computer browser, some mental tabs can be closed immediately, while others need to stay open for a while.

Mindfulness helps you look at these thoughts more intentionally instead of letting them linger in the background.

Step 1: Brain Dump

Grab a sheet of paper (or more) and do a quick brain dump. Write down everything that's occupying mental space in list form. **List it** exactly as it comes to mind.

Do **not** organize the list, or worry about whether something is important or trivial. Just list it.

Step 2: Decide What Each "Tab" Needs

For each item, decide which action fits best.

- ☐ **Do** – This needs action soon.
- ☐ **Schedule** – This can be done at a specific time later.
- ☐ **Write** – This belongs on a list or planner.
- ☐ **Let It Go** – This doesn't actually need attention.

Example:
Item: *Call mom to discuss dad's birthday party.*
Action: *Schedule. It's Monday. I don't need to call Mom till Friday!*

Item: ____

Action: ____

Item: ____
Action: ____

Item: ____
Action: ____

Item: ____
Action: ____

Item: ____
Action: ____

Item: ____
Action: ____

Item: ____
Action: ____

Item: ____
Action: ____

When thoughts remain vague and unresolved, they tend to circle in the background of the mind. By listing them down and giving them a clear place, you reduce the need for your mind to keep holding onto them.

Breaking Free from Digital Distraction

Modern life constantly pulls your attention outward.

Messages arrive. Phones buzz. News updates refresh. Social media feeds update endlessly. At any moment, dozens of digital signals are competing for your attention.

None of these distractions is inherently bad. Technology can help us communicate, learn, work, and stay connected. But the constant stream of input makes it difficult to stay aware of where your attention actually is.

And mindfulness begins with attention.

So, if your attention is constantly being redirected by notifications, alerts, and scrolling loops, it becomes harder to notice your thoughts, your body, and the present moment.

In other words, digital distraction doesn't just interrupt your day. It interrupts your awareness.

This section explores a few ways to reclaim your attention in a digital world that is designed to capture it.

Conscious Consumption

Most digital content is designed to keep you engaged for as long as possible. Algorithms track what you click, watch, save, share, what posts make you comment, and so on. Over time, they learn what captures your attention... and serve you more of it.

That means that when you open an app or website, you're not just choosing what to consume. The platform is also influencing what you see *next*. Without realizing it, you can move from checking one message to scrolling for an hour!

Mindfulness helps interrupt this pattern by bringing awareness back to the moment you begin interacting with digital content.

Instead of asking, *"What should I look at next?"* mindfulness invites a different question: **Why** *should I look at this right now?*

That small question helps you become more deliberate about how you spend your attention.

Exercise 27: Digital Boundaries

This exercise helps you create a few intentional boundaries around your digital habits.

Step 1: Notice Your Current Patterns

Think about your typical day. When do you usually check your phone or digital devices?

- ☐ First thing in the morning
- ☐ During meals
- ☐ Before I sleep
- ☐ When I feel bored or restless
- ☐ While waiting
- ☐ While watching something
- ☐ Other:

____

____

____

Step 2: Choose One Boundary

Select one small boundary you'd like to experiment with.

- ☐ No phone for the first 30 minutes after waking
- ☐ Check email only at specific times
- ☐ No phone during meals
- ☐ Turn off non-essential notifications
- ☐ Check social media only after lunch/dinner
- ☐ No digital device use before bed
- ☐ Other:

____

____

____

My chosen digital boundary for the next three (3) days:

____

____

Check off each day you're able to do your digital boundary.

☐ **Day 1**   ☐ **Day 2**   ☐ **Day 3**

Step 3: Notice the Effect

After trying this boundary for three days, reflect on what you notice. Did your attention feel different?

☐ I feel more relaxed
☐ I feel less anxious
☐ Same
☐ I feel more focused
☐ I feel less easily distracted

Any more realizations during this time?

Example: I realized I wasn't as bothered about missing out on what was happening in the world or with others as I thought I would be.

____

____

____

____

Exercise 28: The "Doomscrolling" Antidote

Doom scrolling happens when you keep scrolling through negative or alarming content even though it makes you feel worse. News headlines, social media debates, and crisis updates can pull your attention deeper and deeper into the scroll.

The mind often does this because it believes more information will create certainty or control. But in reality, it usually increases anxiety instead.

Mindfulness helps you notice the moment when scrolling stops being useful and starts becoming automatic.

Step 1: Recognize the Moment
Think about the last time you found yourself scrolling longer than you intended. What did it feel like?

- ☐ Felt like I lost track of time
- ☐ Felt tense or uneasy
- ☐ Felt unproductive, like I should have been doing something else
- ☐ Felt a bit hopeless about the state of the world
- ☐ Felt "behind" looking at the feeds of other people
- ☐ Other:

____

____

____

Step 2: Interrupt the Scroll

Choose one simple interruption you can use when you notice doom scrolling starting.

- ☐ Put the phone down for two minutes
- ☐ Close my eyes and take three slow breaths
- ☐ Stand up and stretch
- ☐ Close the app
- ☐ Put the phone down and leave the room
- ☐ Journal
- ☐ Step outside
- ☐ Other:

____

____

____

My interruption strategy:

____

____

____

Step 3: Redirect Attention

After interrupting the scroll, gently shift your attention to something else in the present moment. For example, if your interruption strategy is to close your eyes and take three slow breaths, start paying attention to your breathing. If your strategy is to step outside, do a few minutes of Walking Meditation.

Exercise 29: The Digital Purge

A digital purge helps you remove unnecessary digital noise so your mind has fewer things competing for attention. This isn't about eliminating technology from your life. It's about making your digital environment calmer and more intentional.

Step 1: Notice Your Digital Triggers

Take a moment to reflect on how your devices currently affect your attention. Answer the questions below:

When do you find yourself scrolling the most?

Example: At night. I tell myself it's just to help me relax, but then I end up scrolling for 30 minutes to more than an hour.

____

____

____

Which apps tend to pull you in the longest?

Example: Instagram

____

What type of content usually leaves you feeling drained or distracted?

Example: Negative content like the news or something on IG that doesn't show the best side of people.

____

____

____

Are there notifications that interrupt you constantly?

____

____

____

Step 2: Identify What Stays and What Goes

Look through the apps on your phone, tablet, or computer. For each one, ask yourself: *Does this support my life, or does it mostly consume my attention?*

Make two quick lists.

Helpful / Worth Keeping

- _______________________________________

- _______________________________________

- _______________________________________

- _______________________________________

- _______________________________________

Mostly Noise

- _______________________________________

- _______________________________________

- _______________________________________

- _______________________________________

- _______________________________________

Step 3: Take Small Action

Choose one or two simple actions from the list below to reduce digital clutter.

- ☐ Delete one app I rarely use
- ☐ Unfollow accounts that create stress or comparison
- ☐ Turn off non-essential notifications
- ☐ Remove a news app that encourages constant checking
- ☐ Move distracting apps off my Home screen
- ☐ Set a daily time limit for one app
- ☐ Other:

____

____

Step 4: Notice the Effect

After making these changes, pay attention to how your digital environment feels. Reflect after a day or two.

Do I feel less distracted?

____

____

____

Did I notice fewer automatic scrolling moments?

____

____

____

Do I feel "behind" just because I don't know the latest news headlines or what's up with someone?

____

____

____

Note: Digital purges don't need to be dramatic. Even removing one small source of distraction can create more space for attention, calm, and presence in your day.

Intentional Silence

Silence is becoming rare. That's because we've become used to receiving constant input.

Intentional silence simply means choosing moments where you allow things to be quiet. No scrolling. No background media. No constant stimulation.

Just a brief pause where your attention can rest.

Exercise 30: Shhhh!

This exercise invites you to experiment with a small period of intentional silence.

Step 1: Choose a Quiet Window

Pick a short period of time during your day. For example, you can do this while drinking your morning coffee, during a short walk, before going to bed, during part of your commute, etc.

Step 2: Remove Any Digital Input

Put your phone on Silent or leave it in another room.

Step 3: Pick the Length of Quiet Time

How long do you intend to be intentionally quiet? Set a timer for it.

☐ 2 minutes
☐ 5 minutes
☐ 10 minutes

Step 4: Observe Your Experience

On a scale of 1-10, how easy or hard was it to be silent?

1	2	3	4	5	6	7	8	9	10

1 = pretty easy; 10 = very hard

What did you notice during this quiet moment?

Example: I chose 5 minutes, and that was easily doable for me. I actually welcomed the silence, like "At last, some peace and quiet!"

____

____

____

____

____

Did anything change in your attention or mood?

Example: I felt less "scattered."

____

____

____

____

____

Chapter 7: Stop Overthinking & Mental Spirals

Everyone experiences overthinking and mental spirals.

A small thought appears (e.g., something you said earlier, something that might happen tomorrow, something someone said, etc.), and within seconds, your mind starts building a chain of possibilities. One thought leads to another, and before you know it, you're replaying conversations, predicting outcomes, imagining worst-case scenarios, or analyzing the same situation from every possible angle.

This is what we often call **overthinking**.

Overthinking is the mind trying to figure things out, solve problems, or gain certainty. On the surface, it can feel useful; it's a way to be thorough or responsible. But instead of leading to clarity, it often leads to *more* questions, *more* doubt, and *more* mental noise.

When overthinking continues unchecked, it can turn into a **mental spiral**.

A mental spiral is what happens when thoughts start looping and feeding into each other. The tone often shifts from "figuring things out" to feeling stuck, overwhelmed, or anxious. The same thoughts repeat, intensify, and become harder to step away from.

So while overthinking and mental spirals are closely related, you can think of them like this:

- **Overthinking** is the mind trying to solve or analyze.
- **Mental spirals** are what happen when that process loops and escalates.

Now, both are completely normal. In fact, the mind is very good at this.

Our minds evolved to scan for problems and anticipate danger. From a survival standpoint, that ability helped humans prepare for threats long before they arrived.

But in modern life, that same ability often turns inward. Instead of solving a real problem, the mind begins looping through possibilities that may never happen. And the more attention the thought receives, the stronger the spiral becomes.

Over time, this can lead to something many people recognize but rarely name: **mental paralysis**.

You think so much about what to say, what to do, or what might happen that you end up **doing nothing at all**. You feel stuck, drained, and unable to move forward, not because you don't care, but because your mind is overloaded.

This is why learning to interrupt overthinking and mental spirals matters. Not because thinking is bad, but because getting *trapped* in these loops can quietly take away your clarity, energy, and ability to act.

Mindfulness offers a different way of relating to these moments.

Instead of trying to force your thoughts to stop, mindfulness helps you notice when the spiral begins. You learn to pause, observe what the mind is doing, and create a little space between you and the thought.

When you're fully caught inside a mental spiral, every thought feels urgent and believable. But **when you step back and observe** the process, you begin to see something important: **thoughts are just events in the mind, not instructions you must follow**.

In other words, you can notice a thought without automatically chasing it or being attached to it.

The goal of this chapter isn't to eliminate thinking. That's neither possible nor necessary. The goal is to change how you respond when the mind begins to run.

With practice, you'll start to notice spirals earlier. And when you do, you'll learn to pause, observe, and gently redirect your attention (instead of getting pulled deeper into the loop).

Skill 1: Notice the Overthinking Spiral

Overthinking often starts quietly. A single thought appears, and before you realize it, your mind is already several steps ahead. The key is to **notice it early**.

Instead of getting pulled into the content of your thoughts, try to recognize the *pattern*:

I'm replaying this again.
I'm trying to predict everything.
My mind is going in circles.

You're not trying to stop the thought here. You're just naming what's happening → *"This is overthinking."*

That small moment of awareness creates the first bit of space.

Exercise 31: What's Happening?

When your mind begins racing, it can feel like everything is happening at once. This exercise helps you slow down and identify what is actually occurring in the moment.

Step 1: Pause

Take one slow breath. Instead of reacting immediately, simply ask yourself: *What is happening right now?*

Step 2: Separate the Pieces

Write down what you notice in three categories.

Situation (what happened or what triggered the thought):

Example: I heard a song that my ex used to sing to me.

____

____

____

____

Thoughts that appeared:

Example: I was immediately brought back to the pain of breaking up.

____

____

____

____

Feelings or body sensations:

Example: I suddenly felt sad and noticed an ache in my chest.

____

____

____

____

Step 3: Observe the Mind

Take a moment to notice how quickly your mind began connecting thoughts.

What did you notice about how the spiral started?

Example: It seemed to happen pretty fast. I just heard a few notes, and I was suddenly transported back to the breakup.

____

____

____

____

Step 4: Return to the Present

Gently bring your attention back to what is actually happening **right now**. Look around you for a moment.

What's happening in this moment, separate from the thoughts that appeared?

Example: I'm sitting in my car, and a song came on the radio. Nothing else is actually happening right now.

____

____

____

____

Step 5: Reflect

How did separating the situation, thoughts, and feelings change how the moment felt?

Example: It helped me see that what I was experiencing came from memory. The situation itself, although painful, is in the past.

____

____

____

____

Step 6: Grounding Mantra (Optional)

Sometimes it helps to end this exercise with a simple grounding reminder. Quietly repeat a short phrase to yourself as you take one slow breath. Examples:

This is a memory. I'm safe right now.
A thought appeared, I noticed it, and now I'm letting it go.
That moment is in the past. I am HERE now.

Write a phrase that feels natural and calming to you.

____

____

____

____

Exercise 32: Identify the Loop

Many mental spirals follow the same pattern over and over. By recognizing your most common loops, you can begin noticing them earlier.

Step 1: Recall a Recent Spiral

Think about a recent time when your thoughts started circling. What triggered it?

Example: An upcoming family gathering.

____

____

____

Step 2: Map the Thought Pattern

Write your sequence of thoughts as they appeared.

Example:
→ Family gathering this weekend.
→ It's going to be stressful!
→ I'll have to interact with A LOT of relatives.
→ Someone is bound to ask why I still don't have kids.
→ I have to explain myself over and over again.
→ I'll feel uncomfortable.

Now write your own loop:

→ ____

→ ____

→ ____

→ ____

→ _______________________________________

→ _______________________________________

→ _______________________________________

→ _______________________________________

→ _______________________________________

→ _______________________________________

Step 3: Notice the Pattern

What do you observe about how your thoughts developed?

Example: My mind quickly jumped from a family gathering to the most uncomfortable conversations, and I assumed the whole experience would be stressful.

____

____

____

____

____

Awareness is usually the first *interruption* a mental spiral needs. And when you see a pattern, that's often enough for a mental spiral to loosen its grip.

However, not every mental loop needs to be stopped. Sometimes your mind is pointing to something that actually needs attention. If this is the case, proceed to the next step.

Step 4: Decide What This Loop Needs

Ask yourself:

Is this something I can prepare for?

Is this something I can take action on?

Is this something my mind is trying to control, but is in reality out of my control?

Depending on your answer, choose one of the options below.

If Preparation Is Required

Sometimes a loop means you want to feel ready.

My preparation plan:

Example: Remind myself I can change the subject or step away if the conversation becomes uncomfortable.

____

____

____

If Action Is Needed

Write one small step you can take to address the situation.

Example: To lessen my stress, I'll prepare a short response if someone asks about kids, like, "Yep, still no kids. I'll let you know when that changes," or "Yep, still no kids, and I prefer not to discuss this anymore."

My action step:

____

____

____

If It's Outside My Control

Sometimes the mind keeps looping around something that cannot be solved right now. In that case, your task is to notice the loop and gently return to the present moment.

Write a short reminder to yourself:

Example: "I've already thought about this. I'll handle it when the time comes."

____

____

____

Skill 2: Step Back from the Thought

Once you recognize you're starting to overthink, the next step is to create distance from the thought itself.

The mind often treats thoughts as *facts* or *warnings* that must be solved immediately. But mindfulness invites you to observe thoughts instead of wrestling with them.

Remember, a thought can appear, stay for a moment, and pass without needing to be solved.

Exercise 33: Watch, Don't Wrestle

Many people try to *fight* their thoughts. Ironically, the more you struggle against a thought, the more attention it receives. This exercise helps you practice simply observing a thought as it appears.

Step 1: Notice a Thought

Write down a thought that has appeared in your mind recently.
Example: I'm tired of my friend Lily ghosting me!

____

____

____

Step 2: Observe Without Engaging

For a moment, imagine this thought as something separate from you. For example, imagine the thought as:

- a cloud passing through the sky

- a leaf floating down a stream
- a line of text on a screen
- a balloon floating away from you

Step 3: Reflect

What happened when you simply *watched* the thought instead of arguing with it?

Example: I'm not sure why, but somehow, it felt as if the thought had less of a hold on me.

____

____

____

Exercise 34: What This Thought Is Protecting

Many anxious thoughts appear because the mind is trying to protect you. It may be trying to prevent embarrassment, avoid mistakes, or prepare for possible problems.

Understanding the *purpose* behind a thought can sometimes soften its intensity.

Step 1: Choose a Recurring Thought

Write down a thought that often appears when you feel stressed or anxious.

Example: I don't have many friends I can call and hang out with.

____

____

____

____

Step 2: Ask the Question

What might this thought be trying to protect you from?

Example: loneliness

Step 3: Reflect

How does the thought change when you view it as a protective signal rather than a fact?

Example: It helps me see that the thought is really about wanting connection. Instead of treating it like a fact about my life, I can see it as a reminder that I might need more social contact.

Skill 3: Reality-Check the Story

Overthinking often leads to mental spirals because the mind starts building a story about what *might* happen. Mindfulness allows you to pause and examine that story rather than automatically believing it.

Exercise 35: Fact vs. Fear

This exercise helps you separate what you know for certain (facts) from what your mind is imagining.

Step 1: Write the Thought or Situation

What thought or situation is currently causing your mind to spiral?

Example: My finances are keeping me up at night.

____

____

____

____

Step 2: List the Facts

Facts are things you can verify. Examples: what has already happened, observable events, what someone actually said, etc.

Facts:

Example: I have a job right now. I was able to save before. Not the best option, but I CAN call on my sister for some financial help if necessary.

____

____

____

____

Step 3: List the Fear-Based Thoughts

These are interpretations, predictions, or assumptions.

Fear-based thoughts:

Example: I'm worried I might lose my job. I'm anxious that my finances won't improve.

____

____

____

____

Step 4: Notice the Difference

How does it feel to separate facts from imagined outcomes?

Example: It gives me some relief... and hope!

____

____

____

____

Exercise 36: "And Then What?" Anxiety Drill

Anxiety often grows by stacking predictions on top of each other. This exercise helps you follow those predictions all the way through instead of stopping at the most alarming possibility.

Step 1: Write the Fear

What are you worried about?

Example: My husband is cheating.

____

____

____

Step 2: Ask "And Then What?"

Continue asking the same question after each answer.

→ *And then what?*
→ My husband will leave me.
→ *And then what?*
→ Everyone will pity me.
→ *And then what?*
→ I'll be all alone.
→ *And then what?*
→ I'll grow old without anyone caring for me.
→ *And then what?*
→ I'll pass away, and no one will even notice I'm gone.

Now try it with your own concern.

→ ____

→ *And then what?*

→ _______________________________________

→ *And then what?*

→ _______________________________________

→ *And then what?*

→ _______________________________________

→ *And then what?*

→ _______________________________________

→ *And then what?*

→ _______________________________________

→ *And then what?*

→ _______________________________________

→ *And then what?*

Step 3: Reflect

What did you notice as you followed the fear to the end?

Example: I realized my mind was creating a story about the future rather than describing what was actually happening right now.

____

____

____

In the next exercise, you'll take a closer look at the assumptions you make out of fear and explore alternative ways to view your thoughts.

Skill 4: Stop Feeding Overthinking

Overthinking continues because it's being fueled by attention.

Every time you replay, analyze, re-check, or mentally rehearse something, you're giving the thought more energy. And the mind takes that attention as a signal that the thought is important, and so it keeps generating more of it.

This is why overthinking can feel so hard to stop. The more you engage with it, the stronger it becomes.

The shift here is simple, but not always easy: **Realize that you don't need to solve the thought. You need to stop feeding it.**

Instead of trying to figure everything out, practice gently redirecting your attention. For example, you might notice the urge to:

- go over it one more time
- find the "right" answer
- get complete certainty

When you notice this, instead of following that urge, you pause. Then you guide your attention somewhere else, such as back to your breath, back to your body, or back to whatever you were doing before the thought appeared.

This is not a way to avoid the thought, but as a way to stop investing more energy into it.

At first, the mind may pull you back again. That's okay; that's normal.

Just remember that each time you notice it and redirect your attention, you're practicing mindfulness AND you're weakening the loop.

Over time, this is what helps overthinking lose its grip.

Exercise 37: The Overthinking Check (Pause & Reset)

Overthinking can feel automatic. But the moment you notice it, you have a chance to respond differently. Use this quick check to bring awareness and create space.

Step 1: Catch the Moment

What were you just thinking about?

Example: I was replaying a disagreement I've had with my dad earlier today.

____

____

____

Step 2: Name the Pattern

Which of these best describes what's happening?

☐ Replaying the past
☐ Worrying about the future

- ☐ Imagining worst-case scenarios
- ☐ Trying to figure everything out
- ☐ Just going in circles here
- ☐ Other: _______________________________

____

____

Step 3: Check the Impact

How is this affecting you right now?

- ☐ I feel more anxious
- ☐ I feel stuck or unable to act
- ☐ I feel mentally drained
- ☐ I feel emotionally charged
- ☐ No real clarity is coming from this
- ☐ Other: _______________________________

____

____

Step 4: Ground Back to the Present

Gently bring your attention to your breath, your body (feet, hands, posture), and your surroundings.

What did you do?

Example: I did the 10-Breath Reset.

____

____

____

What do you notice right now?

Example: I feel like I created enough distance from my thoughts that I can move forward to something else. I also feel some emotional relief.

____

____

____

Step 5: Choose Your Next Step

Instead of continuing the loop, what's one small, helpful action you can take?

Example: Get a cup of coffee.

____

____

____

Exercise 38: Worst Case, Best Case, Most Likely

The mind often jumps directly to the worst possible outcome. This exercise helps you step back and consider a fuller range of possibilities.

Step 1: Write the Situation

What situation or worry is currently on your mind?

Example: I've been feeling isolated lately and worry that I might end up alone without meaningful friendships.

____

____

____

____

Step 2: Imagine the Worst Case

What is the worst outcome your mind is predicting?

Example: I slowly drift further away from people. I stop getting invited to things and lose contact with friends. Over time, I become completely isolated and spend most of my life alone.

____

____

____

____

Step 3: Imagine the Best Case

Now consider the opposite extreme. What is the best possible outcome?

Example: I reconnect with a friend or meet new people through work or shared activities. Over time, my social life improves, and I feel supported and connected.

Step 4: Consider the Most Likely Outcome

Reality usually falls somewhere between your worst and best case scenarios. What outcome feels most realistic?

Example: I may continue to feel lonely at times, but that doesn't mean permanent isolation. With small efforts like reaching out (instead of waiting to be reached out to), joining activities, or staying open to new connections, my situation could gradually improve.

Step 5: Reflection

What do you notice after looking at all three possibilities?

Example: I noticed that my mind focused only on the worst-case scenarios that I haven't even tried to think of alternatives.

Exercise 39: Overthinking Time Limit

Trying to force yourself to "stop thinking" rarely works. A more effective strategy is to place a time boundary around the thinking process.

Instead of letting your mind spiral for hours, you give the worry a short, contained window.

Step 1: Set a Timer

Choose a short window to think about the issue and set a timer for it.

- ☐ 2 minutes
- ☐ 5 minutes
- ☐ 10 minutes

Step 2: Let Your Mind Work

Allow yourself to think freely about the situation. Don't control or censure your thoughts. Simply let them appear and pass while the timer runs.

Tip: If helpful, briefly jot down one or two key worries that come up on a piece of paper.

Step 3: End the Session

When the timer ends, the thinking session ends too.

Take one slow breath and gently redirect your attention to something else, such as your surroundings, a task, or the next part of your day.

What helped you shift your attention?

Example: I stood up, got myself a cup of coffee, and focused on the next task on my To-Do list.

Part 3: Mindfulness in the Body

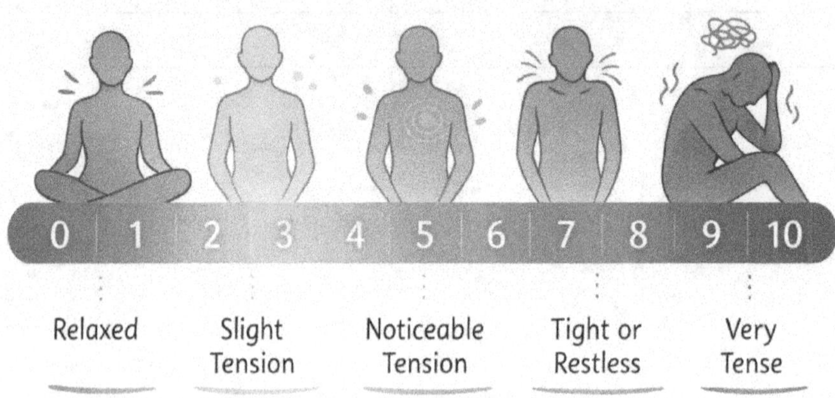

Before you go further, do a quick check in here. Using the image above as a guide, take a few seconds and gently notice your body. Pay attention to areas like your shoulders, jaw, chest, or stomach.

You're not trying to change anything, just notice.

On a scale of 1-10, how does your body feel right now? There's no right or wrong answer. Go with your first impression.

_______ / 10

Chapter 8: Why Your Body Is the Key to Awareness

Most mindfulness advice focuses on the mind. But the body often notices stress long before your thoughts do.

In fact, traditional mindfulness, with its Buddhist roots, was never just "watch your thoughts." It always included body awareness, movement, attention to breathing and posture, walking meditations, and noticing tension in everyday life.

The Western version is the one that shrank mindfulness into a purely mental practice. So in this section, we return to the body as a powerful doorway into awareness. Why?

Because when you learn to notice body signals, you can often catch stress much sooner, *before* it grows into exhaustion, overwhelm, or mental spirals.

Mindfulness in the body means learning to check in earlier. That is, instead of living only in your thoughts, you begin paying attention to what your body is trying to communicate to you throughout the day.

Exercise 40: Interoception Reset

Mindfulness in the body starts with noticing. And **interoception** is your ability to notice what's happening inside your body, such as tension, tightness, restlessness, or ease.

This skill is a core part of many **somatic (body-based) therapies**,[9] where attention to physical sensations is used to help regulate stress and emotions.

In simple terms, interoception means: **listening to your body instead of ignoring it.**

You've already taken a moment to notice where you are on the **Body Awareness Meter** (page 152). Now, the next step is to gently respond to what your body is telling you.

Step 1: Check Your Current State
Write your current number from the Body Awareness Meter:

_____________ / **10**

Step 2: Locate It in Your Body
Where do you feel stress or tension most clearly?

☐ Head
☐ Shoulders
☐ Jaw
☐ Chest
☐ Stomach
☐ Hands
☐ Legs

☐ Other: ___________________________________

Step 3: Name the Sensation (Not the Story)

Instead of explaining why you feel this way, describe the physical sensation. Examples: "Tight," "heavy," "buzzing," "warm," "cold," "restless, "tense," etc.

Describe the sensation:

____

____

Step 4: Choose a Simple Reset

Now ask yourself: *What would help my body feel even 10% better right now?*

Choose a reset:
- ☐ Jaw tension → let your jaw soften.
- ☐ Tense or shallow breathing → take 3–5 slow breaths.
- ☐ Neck/shoulder tension → drop your shoulders slightly.
- ☐ Stomach knows → relax your stomach.
- ☐ Clenched fists → loosen your hands.
- ☐ Restlessness → stand up and walk a few paces.
- ☐ Other:

____

____

____

Don't force relaxation. Just do your chosen reset and allow your body muscles to soften slightly.

Step 5: Check Again

After your reset, notice your body again. How do you feel? What's your new stress or tension number? ________ / **10**

Step 6: Notice the Difference

What feels different after releasing the tension?

Example: I didn't realize how tight my shoulders were until I let them drop. I feel less tense now.

____

____

____

Chapter 9: Why Your Body Feels Exhausted!

In Part 1: Why Life Feels "Too Much," you learned that your body isn't designed to stay in a constant state of alert.

For most of human history, stress appeared in **short bursts**. A threat showed up, the body reacted, and once the danger passed, the system settled again. The heart rate slowed, breathing deepened, muscles relaxed, and the body returned to baseline.

Modern life works very differently. **Today, "threats" are often ongoing pressures that rarely disappear quickly.** Instead, they linger in the background throughout the day.

Because of this, many people live with a body that is permanently on high alert. Our nervous systems are always switched "On."

That's why you feel tired even when you haven't done much physically. The exhaustion you feel is likely due to your body spending long periods in a low-grade stress response.

When the body remains in this always-on mode, it uses energy constantly, so you never fully recharge. Muscles stay partially engaged, the mind stays alert, and your body rarely gets the signal that it's safe to power down fully.

Mindfulness in the body helps interrupt this always-on state. And the first step in interrupting this state is learning to recognize when your body is operating in survival mode.

Exercise 41: Regulation Before Reflection

When you feel stressed or overwhelmed, your first instinct is often to think harder about the problem. But when the body is in a stressed state, the mind rarely finds clear answers. This is because the body is still operating in survival mode.

Before trying to analyze or solve the situation, it often helps to **calm the body first**. When the body settles, the mind usually becomes clearer as well.

This exercise helps you practice regulating the body before reflecting or working on the situation.

Step 1: Recall a Stressful Moment

Think of a recent situation where you felt stressed, overwhelmed, or emotionally triggered.

Example: I received a message from my boss informing me that a project I was in charge of just got canceled, just like that. It really upset me.

____

____

____

____

Step 2: Notice What Happened in Your Body

What physical sensations did you notice in that moment?

Example: My shoulders tensed up immediately, and my thoughts started racing in anger. Looking back now, I think I was also clenching my fists above my keyboard.

Step 3: How Did You React?

Recall what you did in reaction to the stressful moment.

Example: I immediately started typing a reply explaining why the decision was unfair, and how it was a waste of my and my team's time. I copied everyone on my team on the email.

Step 4: What Happened Next?

What was the impact or consequence of your reaction?

Example: My boss called me the next day and asked me if I thought copying all 11 members of my team on my email was "smart." Needless to say, my email escalated the situation, creating more tension between my boss and me.

____

____

____

____

Step 5: Choose a Small Reset

If you paused before reacting, what might have helped calm your body?

Examples: I should have taken three slow breaths or stood up and taken a short walk to calm down.

____

____

____

Step 6: Reflect

How might calming your body first change the way you responded to the situation?

Example: I might have responded more thoughtfully instead of reacting impulsively. For one, I wouldn't have copied all my team members on the email. I realize now that that wasn't necessary.

____

____

____

Takeaway: In the future, try calming your body before analyzing a situation or reacting to it. This simple pause can prevent a stressful moment from escalating.

Chapter 10: Releasing Tension and Resting for Real

In the previous chapter, you explored how the body can become stuck in a low-grade stress response. When this happens, muscles remain partially engaged, breathing becomes shallow, and the body rarely receives the signal that it's safe to relax.

Over time, this tension becomes so familiar that you don't even notice it happening. Tight shoulders, a clenched jaw, or a tense stomach can start to feel like your body's normal state.

Mindfulness in the body helps you recognize physical stress patterns earlier. Why do this?

By learning to notice where tension is stored, you can begin releasing it *before* it builds into deeper exhaustion.

One of the simplest ways to develop this awareness is to get into the habit of doing **body scans**. This practice involves slowly moving your attention through different parts of your body and noticing areas that may be holding tension.

Often, awareness alone allows the body to soften.

Exercise 42: Body Scanning for Tension Release

This exercise will guide you through a simple scan so you can become more aware of where stress is stored in your body.

Step 1: Settle Your Body

Sit comfortably or stand in a relaxed position. *(If time and space allow, you can also lie down.)*

Take one slow breath and allow your shoulders to drop slightly. Don't force anything. Just let your body settle for a moment.

Step 2: Scan From Head to Toe

Slowly bring your attention to each part of your body and notice what you feel. Ask yourself whether the area feels **relaxed**, **neutral**, or **tense**.

Don't rush. Slowly move your attention through your body from head to toe. Scalp → forehead → jaw → neck → shoulders → chest → stomach → lower back → hands → legs → feet.

Which areas feel the most tense right now?

Example: I noticed tightness in my shoulders and jaw.

____

____

____

Pro Tip: Once you get used to body scanning, go even slower and in more detail. For example, don't just scan your forehead, scan your whole face. Forehead → temples → space between eyebrows → eyelids → cheeks → ears → jaw.

Step 3: Gently Release

Choose **one** area where you noticed tension. Take a slow breath and allow that one part of the body to soften slightly.

What area did you try to relax?

Example: My jaw.

____

____

What did you notice after releasing the tension?

Example: I feel less tense and agitated.

____

____

Step 4: Reflect

What did this body scan teach you about where you tend to hold stress?

Example: I didn't realize how often I clench my jaw while working.

____

____

____

____

Exercise 43: Moments of Ease

Mindfulness in the body isn't only about noticing tension. It's also about learning to recognize moments when your body feels **comfortable, calm, or at ease**.

These moments often pass unnoticed because the mind focuses more easily on problems than on neutral or pleasant sensations. So, today, take a moment to remember or notice when your body felt even slightly comfortable.

Step 1: Recall a Recent Moment of Ease

Think of a recent moment when your body felt even slightly comfortable or relaxed. Examples might include:

- Sitting in a comfortable chair
- Taking a warm shower
- Walking outside
- Drinking something warm
- Stretching your back
- Being around someone you feel safe and relaxed with

Write down your moment:

Example: Now that I think about it, when I took some time this morning to get my cup of coffee and sit down and have an unhurried breakfast with my wife, I felt really calm.

____

____

____

____

Step 2: Notice What Your Body Felt Like

What did your **body** feel like in that moment?

Example: My breathing was okay, at least not hurried, and my neck and shoulders were not tense at all. (I usually experience tension in my neck and shoulders.)

____

____

____

____

Step 3: Do More of What Brings Comfort and Ease

What helped create that sense of ease? Was it the activity, the environment, or the people around you?

Example: I truly think it was because I wasn't rushing. Normally, my mind would be racing about work, and I feel like having breakfast was "in the way" of all I had to do.

____

____

____

____

Is there a small way you can create more of this in your day?

Example: Wake up earlier. I spend at least an hour before bed either working or scrolling. I think it's time to limit and eventually stop that habit.

____

____

Step 4: Track Your Moments of Ease

Moments of ease are easy to overlook, but they matter. And although noticing this once is helpful, noticing it *repeatedly* is what creates change.

So, for the next few days, take a moment to notice when your body feels even slightly at ease. Keep it simple, just jot it down.

Moment or Situation	What Did Your Body Feel Like?	Who Were You With (if anyone)?

Moment or Situation	What Did Your Body Feel Like?	Who Were You With (if anyone)?

As you fill out the above tables, **look for patterns**.

Do certain activities help your body relax?
Do certain environments feel calmer?
Are there people you feel more at ease around?

The goal isn't to chase these moments, but to **recognize what already supports your sense of ease**. Over time, you'll find that feeling at ease isn't as rare as you think. They show up in small, everyday moments.

The important thing is that you notice these moments and make an effort to experience more of them.

Micro-Rest for Busy People

When people think about rest, they often imagine something big: a vacation, a full day off, a long nap, or an hour-long meditation. But real life rarely gives us that much space.

Most days are filled with responsibilities, deadlines, conversations, and digital distractions. Because of this, many people move from task to task without ever allowing their bodies to reset. The result is a gradual buildup of tension and fatigue.

Fortunately, **rest doesn't always require long breaks.** The body can begin to reset in very small windows of time. These short pauses are called micro-rests.

A micro-rest is a brief moment where you intentionally soften the body, slow your breathing, or step away from mental pressure. These pauses may only last a few seconds or a minute, but they help prevent stress from continuously building throughout the day.

Instead of waiting until you're completely exhausted, micro-rests allow you to release small amounts of tension regularly.

The following exercises will show you how to use short pauses during your day to reset your body and restore a little energy.

Exercise 44: 10-Second Reset

This exercise teaches you how to use tiny resets throughout the day, especially when you feel pressure building.

Step 1: PAUSE

When you notice stress or tension rising, pause for a moment. You don't need to leave what you're doing. Simply stop or freeze your actions for about 10 seconds.

Step 2: Reset the Body

Gently do the following:

- Take one slow breath.
- Drop your shoulders slightly.
- Unclench your jaw.
- Relax your hands.

That's it.

Step 3: Continue Your Day

After this brief reset, return to what you were doing.

You don't need to feel completely calm. The goal is simply to interrupt the *buildup* of tension before it grows stronger.

When could you try a 10-second reset today?

Example: Before opening my inbox in the morning.

____

____

Exercise 45: 60-Second Reset

Okay, sometimes your body needs slightly more than ten seconds to settle. If this is what you feel you need, try the following.

Step 1: PAUSE for One Minute

Find a moment during your day when you can pause for about sixty seconds. You can remain seated, standing, or even walk slowly.

Step 2: SLOW DOWN Your Breathing

Take several slow breaths. Notice the movement of your breathing in your chest or stomach. Allow your exhale to be slightly longer than your inhale.

Step 3: RELAX Your Body

As you breathe, note an area (e.g., neck, shoulders, jaw, hands, etc.) that's holding even a bit of tension. Allow this area to soften slightly as you exhale.

What did you notice after the one-minute reset?

Example: My breathing slowed down.

____

____

When would a one-minute reset be beneficial during your day?

Example: After finishing a long task or before a meeting.

____

____

Exercise 46: Rest Without Lying Down

Many people believe that rest only happens when you lie down or sleep. But your body can rest even while sitting or standing. In fact, learning to relax the body while remaining awake and active is an important mindfulness skill.

Step 1: Notice Your Current Posture

Pause and notice how you're sitting or standing.

Are your shoulders raised or hunched forward?
Are you scrunching or squinting your eyes together?
Is your jaw tight?
Are you gritting your teeth?
Is your breathing shallow?
Are your fists clenched?

Write down what you notice.

____

____

____

Step 2: Allow the Body to Soften

Gently make small adjustments. For example, if your fists are clenched, inhale slowly. And then, as you exhale, slowly open your hands as if you're gently setting a small bird free from your palms. Stay in this position for about 20–30 seconds.

Exercise 47: Micro-Breaks at Work

During busy days, people often work for long periods without stepping away. This can cause tension to build in the body and mind. This micro-break can help you reset before stress accumulates.

A Note on Sitting

You may have heard the phrase, **sitting is the new smoking**. Some people think that's a bit dramatic, is it?

Numerous studies show that sitting for long periods can cause obesity, affect your posture (causing bone and mobility problems), create cardiovascular problems, and even negatively affect your mental health.[10,11,12]

When you sit for long periods without moving, your body becomes stiffer, your circulation slows down, and tension builds up, especially in your neck, shoulders, and lower back.

Over time, this can leave you feeling more tired, more tense, and less focused. The good news is that you don't need to make big changes. You just need to **interrupt long periods of sitting.**

Think of it this way: It's not sitting that's the problem. It's **sitting for too long without a break.**

So instead of staying in one position for hours, give your body regular chances to move... with micro-breaks!

Step 1: Identify a Transition Point

Think about natural transition moments during your day. For example:

- After sending an email
- After finishing a task
- Before starting a meeting
- After a phone call

Which moments in your day could become an opportunity for micro-breaks?

____

____

____

Step 2: Choose a Simple Reset

Select what you want to do during your micro-break.

☐ **Stand + Stretch Up**

Stand up and reach your arms overhead.
Hold for 5–10 seconds and take a slow breath.

☐ **Shoulder Rolls**

Roll your shoulders forward 5 times, then backward 5 times.
Let your neck stay relaxed.

☐ **Neck Reset**

Gently tilt your head side to side.
Don't force it—just ease into the stretch.

☐ **Walk for 30–60 Seconds**
Stand up and take a short walk (even just around the room).
The goal is movement, not distance.

☐ **Open Your Chest**
Clasp your hands behind your back and gently open your chest. This helps counter the "hunched over" position.

☐ **Shake It Out**
Shake your hands, arms, and shoulders loosely.
Let your body release built-up tension.

☐ **Posture Reset**
Stand tall and realign your posture:
- Consciously plant your feet on the ground.
- Roll back and relax your shoulders.
- Tuck your chin slightly.
- Unclench your jaw.
- Hold for a few breaths.

☐ **Wall Support Stretch**
Place your hands on a wall and lean slightly forward.
Feel a stretch through your back and shoulders.

☐ **Mini Squats (or Sit-to-Stand)**
Do 5–10 slow squats, or simply stand up and sit down a few times. Keep it controlled and easy.

☐ **Step Away + Breathe**
Step away from your workspace. (Do **not** check your phone. The goal is to look away from a screen.)
Take at least 3 slow breaths and let your eyes relax.

Note: You don't need to do all of the above. Just pick 1–2 every hour. The goal isn't a full workout. It's to **break the pattern of staying still for too long** and give your body small resets throughout the day.

Which one did you do today?

Example: Step away + breathe.

____

____

____

What did you notice after the micro-break?

Example: I noticed that my thoughts slowed down.

____

____

____

Chapter 11: Movement as Medicine (Without Overdoing It)

Throughout this section, you learned how to notice tension in your body and how small pauses can help interrupt the buildup of stress. But awareness and micro-rest are only part of the picture.

**Sometimes the body doesn't need stillness.
It needs movement.**

When stress builds up, your body often stores that energy in tightened muscles, restless legs, or a sense of agitation. Sitting still and thinking about it rarely releases that energy. It's movement that helps the body complete the stress cycle.

You may have noticed this instinctively. When people feel overwhelmed, they often feel the urge to walk, stretch, pace the room, or shake out their hands. These small movements allow the body to release tension that has been building up.

The goal here isn't intense exercise or performance. Instead, the goal is simple: **move the body in a mindful way so tension has somewhere to go.**

The exercises in this chapter will help achieve just that.

Exercise 48: Moving Stress Out of the Body

This exercise invites you to use simple physical movement to help your body reset.

Step 1: Notice Your Energy

Pause for a moment and check in with your body. Does your body feel:

- ☐ Restless
- ☐ Tense
- ☐ Heavy
- ☐ Low in energy
- ☐ Too high in energy
- ☐ Other:

____

____

Write down what you notice.

Example: I feel low in energy. As a result, I don't feel like doing anything, which makes me feel guilty.

____

____

____

Step 2: Choose a Simple Movement

Choose a movement that matches what your body needs right now.

- ☐ Stand up and walk around the room.

- ☐ Stretch your arms.
- ☐ Roll your shoulders.
- ☐ Shake out your hands.
- ☐ Lie down and do some light yoga.
- ☐ Go out and take a walk.
- ☐ Other:

____

____

Do you need more? If your body still feels restless, stuck, or full of pent-up energy, you may need something more active:

- ☐ March or jog in place.
- ☐ Do 10–15 squats.
- ☐ Do 10–15 lunges (alternating legs)/
- ☐ Do a quick burst of fast walking (or light jogging)
- ☐ Do a few jumping jacks.
- ☐ Walk up and down the stairs.
- ☐ Do wall push-ups.
- ☐ Go out and go for a run.
- ☐ Lymphatic jump (i.e., stand and gently bounce in place) for 30-60 seconds.
- ☐ Do a short "shake + stomp" (i.e., shake your arms while lightly stomping your feet).
- ☐ Do a quick dance to a song or part of a song.
- ☐ Other:

____

____

Whatever you do, don't force anything or follow a strict routine. Simply allow your body to move and release tension.

Step 4: Reflect

What did you notice in your body after moving?

Example: I walked around the neighborhood for 25 minutes. I feel invigorated!

____

____

____

____

____

Exercise 49: Mindful Stretching

Stretching can help release physical tension while bringing your attention back into the body. Unlike exercise focused on performance, mindful stretching emphasizes awareness and gentle movement.

Step 1: Choose a Simple Stretch

Select a stretch that feels comfortable for your body.

- ☐ Stretching your arms overhead.
- ☐ Roll your neck gently.
- ☐ Stretching your back.
- ☐ Reach your arms forward → upward → forward → downward.
- ☐ Other:

____

____

Step 2: Move Slowly

Perform the stretch slowly and gently. As you move, notice:

- how your muscles feel
- where you feel tightness
- how your breathing changes

Allow the movement to remain comfortable and controlled.

Step 3: Breathe and Hold

Hold the stretch for a few breaths. Allow your breathing to remain slow and natural.

Step 4: Reflect

What did you notice while stretching?

Example: I noticed tightness in my shoulders that slowly started to release.

____

____

____

____

Pro Tip: Stretching is an effective way to release tension and support your body. Research suggests that regular stretching can improve flexibility and reduce muscle tightness[13,14], especially if you've been sitting for long periods.

When can you fit a short but regular stretching routine in your day?

Example: At night works best for me. After I put the kids to sleep, I'll spend 5–10 minutes stretching before I go downstairs and finish a few things.

____

____

____

____

Exercise 50: Transition Reset

Throughout the day, you move from one activity to another—finishing a task, leaving a meeting, ending a phone call, or switching from work to home life.

However, the body often carries the tension from one situation into the next. In Activity 25: Transition Pauses, you applied breathwork. In this exercise, you'll use a short movement reset between activities to help release that built-up tension.

Step 1: Notice a Transition Moment

Think about a common transition in your day. Examples:

- walking through a doorway
- finishing one task before starting another
- entering your home after work
- opening a new email or message
- entering a room before a meeting
- ending a phone call
- arriving home after work

What transition could you use as a reset moment?

Example: After finishing a long task at my desk.

____

____

____

Step 2: Choose a Small Movement

During that transition, pick a movement you can do for a few seconds.

- ☐ Stretch your arms overhead.
- ☐ Roll your shoulders.
- ☐ Shake out your hands.
- ☐ Move your neck side-to-side.
- ☐ Stand up and walk briefly.
- ☐ Other:

____

____

Step 3: Reflect

How might adding a short movement reset help your body throughout the day?

Example: I think it could prevent tension from building up during long periods at my desk.

____

____

____

Part 4: Opening to Gratitude

When you live with gratitude,

life meets you with more of it.

-LifeZen

GRATITUDE

Chapter 12: Shifting the Lens to Gratitude

The world often feels heavy.

News cycles are relentless. Work pressures pile up. Relationships can be complicated. Some days it may seem like life is mostly about solving problems and just surviving the day.

When things feel uncertain, messy, or overwhelming, the idea of gratitude can even sound unrealistic. You might think, *"What exactly am I supposed to feel grateful for right now?"*

Gratitude is often misunderstood as pretending everything is fine or forcing yourself to focus only on the positive. However, **real gratitude doesn't ignore difficulty, pain, or frustration. It simply invites you to widen the lens of your attention.**

When the mind is under pressure, it naturally scans for problems. That isn't a personal flaw; it's part of how the brain evolved to keep us safe. We become very good at noticing what is wrong, what might go wrong, and what still needs to be fixed.

Over time, this constant *problem-scanning* can make the world feel heavier than it actually is.

Gratitude gently shifts that pattern.

It doesn't erase problems, but it helps you notice that other things are also present, small moments of support, brief experiences of ease, and quiet signals that life contains more than just stress.

Opening to gratitude means learning to notice those moments again.

In this section, you'll explore a different way of seeing your experiences. Instead of forcing positivity, you'll learn how appreciation can exist *alongside* difficulty, uncertainty, and imperfection.

Gratitude isn't about denying the hard parts of life. It's about recognizing that even amidst the mess and noise, something worthwhile can still be found.

The Neuroscience of Appreciation

Your brain is constantly learning from what you repeatedly notice.

Every time you focus on something, whether it's a problem, a worry, or a positive experience, your brain strengthens the neural pathways connected to that pattern of attention. Over time, this creates habits of perception. The brain becomes faster and more efficient at noticing the same kinds of things again!

Because the human brain evolved to keep us safe, it's naturally very good at spotting problems, threats, and potential risks. That's often called the **negativity bias**. Your brain is designed to remember what went wrong so it can avoid danger in the future.

The downside is that this can make the mind feel like a **problem detector** that rarely switches off.

Practicing appreciation gently shifts that pattern.

When you regularly notice things that are going well—small successes, moments of calm and ease, times of support, or simple pleasures—you begin strengthening a different set of neural pathways. The brain becomes better at recognizing these signals, just as it becomes skilled at detecting problems. Over time, appreciation becomes easier and more natural.

And that is where gratitude and mindfulness naturally connect.

Mindfulness helps you slow down and notice what is already present.

Gratitude builds on that awareness by helping you recognize what in that moment might be meaningful, supportive, or worthwhile.

In other words, mindfulness opens your attention. Gratitude helps shape what you begin to notice within that wider awareness.

Together, they train the brain to see a more complete picture of your experience.

Exercise 51: Small Wins

The brain tends to focus on unfinished tasks, mistakes, and problems that still need solving. Because of this, many positive moments pass by unnoticed.

This exercise will help you tune in to everyday moments that show progress, effort, or something going slightly better than expected.

Training your attention to notice these moments helps your brain build new pathways for appreciation.

Step 1: Recall a Small Win

Think about something that went well today or recently. It doesn't have to be a big achievement. Small wins might include:

- waking up on time
- finishing a task
- having a supportive conversation
- completing something you had been putting off
- taking care of yourself in a small way

What's your small win today?

Example: I finally sent an email I had been procrastinating on.

____

____

____

Step 2: Notice What Made It a Win

Why did this moment matter to you?

Example: I had been avoiding it for days, so finishing it felt like progress.

____

____

____

Step 3: Pause and Acknowledge It

Take a moment to recognize the effort or progress behind this small win. What did this moment say about your effort, persistence, or values?

Example: It reminded me that I can follow through even when something feels uncomfortable.

____

____

____

You know, **small wins happen more often than you realize.** So why not track them over the next few days?

Day 1
Small Win

What Happened?

How Did It Feel?

Day 2

Small Win

What Happened?

How Did It Feel?

Day 3

Small Win

What Happened?

How Did It Feel?

Day 4

Small Win

What Happened?

How Did It Feel?

Day 5

Small Win

What Happened?

How Did It Feel?

Day 6

Small Win

What Happened?

How Did It Feel?

Day 7

Small Win

What Happened?

How Did It Feel?

Hard & Easy + Bad & Good

One of the biggest misunderstandings about gratitude is the belief that you must choose between acknowledging what is difficult and appreciating what is good.

In reality, both can exist at the same time.

Life rarely falls neatly into categories of *good* or *bad*. A situation can be frustrating and meaningful. A day can be stressful and still contain moments of connection or progress. Something can feel disappointing while also teaching you something valuable.

The mind often tries to simplify experiences into one label: *This day was terrible,* or *This situation is great.* But most real experiences are more complex than that.

Learning to hold **both sides of an experience** is an important mindfulness skill. Why?

Because doing so helps you realize that your experience may contain more than one truth at the same time.

The following exercise will help you practice holding these two perspectives together.

Exercise 52: Both Are True

This exercise will help you explore how two seemingly opposite truths can both be valid.

Step 1: Describe a Difficult Situation

Think of a situation in your life that feels challenging, frustrating, or disappointing.

Example: My workload has been overwhelming lately.

____

____

____

Step 2: Acknowledge the Difficult Part

Write down what feels difficult about this situation.

Example: I feel constant pressure and worry that I will fall behind.

____

____

____

Step 3: Look for Another Truth

Now consider whether there is another perspective or element within the same situation that might also be true.

Example: Even though the workload is stressful, it also shows that my work is trusted and valued.

____

____

____

Step 4: Hold Both Together

Write the two truths side by side.

MY TWO TRUTHS		
My workload is overwhelming.	**AND**	*My work is valued.*
	AND	
	AND	
	AND	
	AND	
	AND	
	AND	
	AND	

Exercise 53: Micro-Joys in the Mess

Life is rarely perfectly calm or organized. Most days include a mix of responsibilities, stress, and unexpected challenges.

Yet even during messy or stressful days, small moments of comfort, relief, or enjoyment often appear. These are micro-joys, brief experiences that bring a small sense of ease or appreciation.

This exercise helps you practice noticing these moments.

Step 1: Recall a Challenging Day

Think of a recent day that felt stressful, busy, or frustrating.

Example: Yesterday was overwhelming because I had multiple deadlines and felt behind on everything.

____

____

____

Step 2: Look for Micro-Joys

Even on difficult days, small positive moments often appear. Examples might include:

- a warm cup of coffee
- a kiss or hug from someone
- a supportive message from someone
- a short moment of quiet
- finishing one small task

- hearing something that made you smile

What small moments of ease or appreciation appeared during that day?

Example: A coworker thanked me for helping them with a problem.

____

____

____

Step 3: Notice the Contrast

How did noticing these small moments affect your experience of the day?

Example: The day was still stressful, but that moment reminded me that not everything was going wrong.

____

____

____

Exercise 54: Gratitude in Action (Pay It Forward)

Gratitude isn't just something you feel. It's something you can express. When you actively share appreciation, through words, actions, or small gestures, it doesn't just benefit others. It reinforces your own awareness of what's good.

This is often called **paying it forward**. You notice something positive... and then you pass it on.

Interestingly, research shows that kindness tends to spread. When you extend it, it often comes back, either directly or through the way it influences others.[15,16]

Step 1: Notice Something You Appreciate

Think of something (or someone) you appreciate today.

Example: I was carrying shopping bags and a big cup of coffee from a nearby café. As I got into the elevator, I realized that the coffee was TOO HOT! I had to set it down on the floor.

As the elevator doors opened on my floor, a stranger who was about to come in saw my predicament, quickly took a handkerchief out, picked up the coffee from the floor, and held the elevator doors open for me to get out. He then accompanied me right up to my door. We laughed all the time, and I thanked him profusely!

____

____

____

____

____

Step 2: Pay It Forward

Choose one simple way to express your appreciation. This could be towards the same person or someone else. It doesn't have to be big or perfect.

What will you do?

Example: Going in and out of elevators is so impersonal. From now on, I intend to pay appreciation for that moment forward by SMILING at people I come across in elevators.

____

____

____

____

____

Step 3: Keep It Going!

Gratitude grows when you use it. For the next few days, try to notice one thing each day and express it in some way, even if it's small.

You're not forcing positivity here. You're training your attention to recognize and extend what's already there.

What I'm Grateful For	How I'm Going to Pay This Forward

What I'm Grateful For	How I'm Going to Pay This Forward

Chapter 13: Letting Go of the Fight Inside Your Mind

In Chapter 3: Mindfulness in Plain English, we mentioned that mindfulness is the doorway to acceptance. In many ways, this simply means **allowing what is already present**.

This can feel surprisingly difficult.

When something unpleasant happens, the mind's natural reaction is to **fight the experience**. We try to push the feeling away, argue with reality, or mentally replay the situation in an attempt to change what has already happened.

You may notice thoughts like:

This shouldn't be happening.
Why is this happening to me?
I need to fix this right now.

This reaction is understandable. The brain is wired to solve problems and protect us from discomfort. When something feels wrong, the mind immediately tries to correct it.

The challenge is that many situations in life cannot be solved instantly. Difficult emotions, disappointments, uncertainty, and frustration are part of the human experience. When we constantly fight these realities, we often create **a second layer of suffering**.

The original situation may already be difficult. But the mental struggle against it—arguing with it, resisting it, wishing it were different—adds even more tension.

Mindfulness offers another approach.

Instead of fighting the experience, you practice **softening toward it**.

Allowing doesn't mean liking what's happening, giving your approval, or surrendering. It simply means acknowledging what is already present without immediately resisting it.

For example, instead of saying *"This is wrong. I shouldn't feel this way,"* you might notice *"Okay, I don't like it, but this is what I'm feeling right now."*

Instead of immediately trying to eliminate the discomfort, you give the experience a little space to exist.

This small shift can be powerful. When you stop fighting the moment, the body often relaxes slightly. The mind becomes less reactive, and you gain more clarity about how to move forward.

In this sense, allowing isn't passive. It is a form of **mental flexibility**.

Rather than exhausting yourself by resisting reality, you begin working **with the moment as it is**. And from that place, wiser and calmer responses become possible.

The following exercises will help you explore what it means to soften your resistance and practice allowing difficult experiences without being overwhelmed by them.

Exercise 55: Allowing Without Fixing

This exercise helps you explore what it means to soften your resistance and practice allowing difficult experiences without being overwhelmed by them.

Step 1: Recall a Difficult Moment

Think of a recent moment when something felt uncomfortable, frustrating, or upsetting.

Example: I received criticism about my report and immediately felt defensive.

____

____

____

Step 2: Notice the Urge to Fix the Situation

What did your mind want to do right away?

Example: I wanted to defend myself and explain why the criticism was unfair. I wanted to say that my report was right and should stay that way.

____

____

____

Step 3: Practice Allowing

Imagine pausing for a moment before reacting.

What might it look like to simply acknowledge the experience?

Example: I might notice, "I feel hurt and defensive right now," without trying to respond immediately.

____

____

____

Step 4: Give the Moment Space

If you allowed the feeling to exist for a short time, what might change?

Example: The feeling might still be uncomfortable, but it may become less intense once I stop fighting it.

____

____

____

Sometimes clarity appears only after the mind stops struggling. Allowing an experience to simply exist, _even briefly_, can create the space needed for a calmer and wiser response.

Self-Compassion as a Shield

One of the most important things mindfulness teaches is how to **notice the voice inside your mind**.

When something goes wrong, many people automatically turn that voice against themselves. The mind quickly produces harsh judgments:

I should have done better.
Why do I always mess things up?
Everyone else seems to handle this better than I do.

These thoughts often appear so quickly that we barely question them. They simply feel like the truth.

Mindfulness helps you slow down enough to **hear that inner dialogue more clearly**. And instead of being carried away by that internal critic, you begin to recognize it as just another pattern of thinking.

Once you notice the tone of that voice, you can choose how you want to respond. This is where **self-compassion** comes in.

Self-compassion isn't about ignoring mistakes or pretending everything is fine. It means responding to yourself with the same understanding you would offer a friend who's struggling.

When mindfulness and self-compassion work together, something important happens. You stop automatically attacking yourself during difficult moments. Instead, you create a small space where kindness and perspective can enter.

In this sense, self-compassion acts like a **shield**. It protects you from turning every challenge into self-criticism and allows you to face difficult moments with greater patience and resilience.

Exercise 56: New Inner Script

This activity helps you begin reshaping the way you speak to yourself when things don't go as planned.

Step 1: Notice the Critical Thought

Think of a recent moment when you were hard on yourself.

Example: I was out running in the woods and slipped badly. As I stood up and looked at my own bloody knee, I thought, "Why am I so clumsy!"

____

____

____

____

Step 2: Pause and Observe

Take a moment to look at the thought with curiosity. Ask yourself:

Is this a fact, or is this your mind reacting to a difficult moment?

Example: This was my mind reacting to a difficult moment.

____

____

____

____

What do you notice when you look at the thought this way?

Example: I realized the thought appeared quickly because I was annoyed at seeing my wound and that my run was potentially "ruined."

____

____

____

____

Step 3: Imagine Speaking to a Friend

If a close friend experienced the same situation, how might you respond to them?

Example: Wow, sounds serious. Are you okay?

____

____

____

____

Step 4: Create a New Inner Script

Now try expressing a more supportive response to yourself.

Write your new inner script.

Example: I fell, I got hurt, this can happen to anyone who runs in the woods.

____

____

____

____

Step 5: Reflect

How does the new inner script feel compared to the original thought?

Example: Honestly, I don't know why I'm always so hard on myself, but I am. This new inner script is giving me a new way to be kinder to myself.

____

____

____

____

Why Being Human Is Enough

Many people move through life with the quiet feeling that they should be doing more, achieving more, or handling things better than they currently are.

In a world that constantly measures productivity, success, and performance, it's easy to believe that your worth depends on how much you accomplish or how well you manage every challenge. And when things become overwhelming, the mind often turns that pressure inward:

I should be able to handle this.
Why am I struggling so much?
Other people seem to manage better than I do.
Why haven't I achieved what I want in life yet?

One of the most important insights mindfulness offers is the simple recognition that **you're a human being, not a machine**.

Human beings get tired. They become overwhelmed. They make mistakes. They experience doubt, frustration, and emotional ups and downs.

These experiences are not signs that something is wrong with you or how you live your life. They are signs that you're **living a human life** in a complex and demanding world.

Learning to forgive yourself for moments of overwhelm, even of failure, is an important form of self-compassion. Instead of criticizing yourself for struggling, mindfulness invites you to pause and recognize the reality of the moment.

Sometimes the most supportive response is simply acknowledging: *This is difficult, and it makes sense that I feel this way.*

When you allow yourself to be human, with limitations, emotions, and moments of uncertainty, you begin to soften the constant internal pressure to prove your worth.

In that space, a different understanding can emerge: **Being human, as you are right now, is enough.**

Exercise 57: "This Is Enough" Reflection

This exercise invites you to pause and reflect on the idea that **what you're doing and experiencing right now may already be enough**.

Step 1: Notice the Pressure

Think about an area of your life where you often feel pressure to do more or be better.

Example: Motherhood. I often feel like I should be more organized and "put together" as a mom.

____

____

____

Step 2: Acknowledge the Effort

Now consider what you're already doing in this area. What efforts, responsibilities, or challenges are you currently managing?

Example: I'm showing up every day, no matter what I feel. I'm taking care of my household (partner and two kids), doing meal planning, cooking, driving the kids where they need to be, and keeping track of everyone's schedules (appointments, school activities, and even plans with friends).

____

____

____

Step 3: The Statement

Write a statement that acknowledges your effort while allowing yourself to be human.

Example: I'm doing my best with the time and energy I have right now.

____

____

____

Step 4: Reflect

How does it feel to recognize that what you're doing right now is already enough?

Example: Didn't really realize I needed that validation until I gave it to myself. It feels good, very good.

____

____

____

In this moment, as you are, this is enough.

Part 5: Living with Mindfulness & Lightness in a Heavy World

The world may still be loud, messy, and unpredictable.

But now...
you don't get lost in it.

-LifeZen

Chapter 14: Building a Life that Feels Calmer & More Intentional

Mindfulness isn't just something you practice during an exercise or a quiet moment. Over time, it becomes a way of living.

Many people begin their mindfulness journeys by learning how to pause, notice their thoughts, or calm their bodies during stressful moments. These skills are important, but the **deeper transformation happens when mindfulness begins to shape how you move through your everyday life.**

In a world that constantly pushes for more speed, more productivity, and more attention, living mindfully often means doing something simple but powerful: **creating space**.

Space to breathe.
Space to pause.
Space to notice.
Space to choose your response instead of reacting automatically.

Without intentional space, the day easily fills itself with noise, obligations, and constant stimulation. Emails arrive, messages demand attention, and responsibilities pile up. Before long, the day feels like something that's happening to you rather than something you're consciously participating in.

A mindful life means learning how to gently reclaim parts of your time, energy, and attention. How?

Often it begins with small shifts like protecting moments of quiet, setting boundaries around your energy, and choosing where your attention truly belongs.

Creating Space in Your Day

Mindfulness grows in the presence of space.

When every minute of the day is filled with activity, the mind rarely has time to settle. Thoughts rush from one task to the next, and the body remains in a constant state of motion.

Creating space means allowing brief pauses within the flow of your day. These pauses may be small, like taking a breath before responding to a message, stepping outside for a moment of fresh air, or sitting quietly for a few minutes before starting the next task.

Over time, these small pockets of space become moments where awareness can return.

Instead of moving through the day on autopilot, you begin to experience your life with greater presence.

> **Create "Space" Now**
> *Select ANY activity in this book and do it right now.*

Designing Calm Into Chaos

Modern life often feels chaotic. Schedules shift, demands appear unexpectedly, and not every situation can be controlled.

While you cannot remove all chaos from your environment, you can intentionally design small elements of calm into your routine. This might include:

- starting your morning without immediately checking your phone
- taking a brief walk after lunch
- creating a quiet moment before going to bed
- allowing a few minutes of stillness between activities
- using an app to remind you to stand up every 45 minutes

These simple habits act like anchors throughout the day. They provide brief moments where the mind can reset before moving into the next task.

When these anchors are repeated consistently, they create a rhythm of calm that helps balance the natural busyness of life.

Decide Now

What small moment of calm do you intend to include in your daily routine? Be specific.

WHAT: _______________________________________

WHERE: _______________________________________

WHEN: _______________________________________

Protecting Your Energy

Your attention and energy are limited resources.

Every conversation, task, responsibility, and digital interaction uses some portion of that energy. When too many demands compete for your attention, exhaustion often follows.

Mindfulness helps you become more aware of **where your energy is going**.

Some activities leave you feeling engaged and fulfilled. Others may drain your energy without offering much in return.

Protecting your energy doesn't mean avoiding responsibilities or withdrawing from others. It simply means becoming more intentional about where you invest your time and attention.

By noticing what supports your well-being, and what repeatedly drains it, you can begin making small adjustments that protect your mental and emotional resources.

Exercise 58: Energy Boundaries Map

This exercise helps you map out the activities and situations that affect your energy the most.

Step 1: Identify Energy Drainers

Think about the activities, responsibilities, or situations that tend to leave you feeling mentally or emotionally drained. This might include:

- constant notifications or messages
- long meetings or work calls
- certain conversations or social situations
- multitasking for long periods
- spending too much time online
- certain people

What situations or activities tend to drain your energy?

Example: Checking emails constantly throughout the day makes me feel mentally scattered.

____

____

____

Step 2: Identify Energy Supporters

Now think about the moments or activities that help restore your energy or bring a sense of calm. Examples might include:

- taking a short walk
- quiet time in the morning

- listening to music
- meaningful conversations
- being in nature

What activities help replenish your energy?

Example: Taking a short walk outside helps me reset.

____

____

____

Step 3: Notice the Pattern

Look at the two lists. What patterns do you notice about what drains and what supports your energy?

Example: I noticed that work emails drain my energy, while anything outdoor-related replenishes it.

____

____

____

Step 4: Choose One Boundary

Consider one small boundary you could introduce to protect your energy.

What boundary would you like to try?

Example: I'd like to stop checking emails after 5 PM.

____

____

____

Saying No Without Guilt

One of the most challenging boundaries for many people is learning how to say no.

Many of us are taught to be helpful, agreeable, and available to others. While these qualities can strengthen relationships, they can also lead to a habit of overcommitting.

When you say yes to every request, obligation, or opportunity, your time and energy quickly become stretched thin.

Mindfulness encourages a different approach.

Before responding automatically, you pause and ask yourself a simple question: *Is this something I genuinely have the time and energy for right now?*

Sometimes the answer will be yes. Other times, the healthiest response may be to decline.

Saying no doesn't mean you are selfish or unkind. It means you are respecting the limits of your time and energy. In many cases, **a thoughtful no is more honest and sustainable than an exhausted yes**.

Exercise 59: Saying "No"

Often, replenishing your energy simply means saying "No" more often. This exercise will help you practice responding with greater clarity.

Step 1: Notice a Recent Request

Think of a recent situation where someone asked for your time, help, or attention.

Example: My sister-in-law asked me to babysit my two nephews for the third time this month.

____

____

____

Step 2: Notice Your First Reaction

What was your immediate instinct?

Example: I felt compelled to say yes, even though I was already feeling overwhelmed with my own kids.

____

____

____

Step 3: Check In With Your Energy

Looking back, did you realistically have the time or energy to take on this request?

Example: No, I was already juggling several deadlines. I was exhausted.

____

____

____

____

Step 4: Practice a Mindful Response

Imagine responding again, this time with greater awareness of your limits. Write a response that respects your time and energy.

Write your response:

Example: I'm not able to take that on right now.

____

____

____

Step 5: Reflect

How might saying "No" more often affect your energy and well-being?

Example: It will give me more time for myself. Instead of rushing between things I have to do for my own family and others, I can take a moment to breathe and not feel constantly pressured.

____

____

____

Staying Steady When Things Go Wrong

No matter how mindful you become, things will still go wrong. That's just life.

Plans fall apart. Problems appear (or reappear). People say things that upset you. Some days simply feel heavier than others.

Mindfulness doesn't prevent these moments. Instead, it helps you develop the ability to **remain steady when challenges appear**.

Instead of being immediately pulled into frustration, worry, or self-criticism, mindfulness helps you return to something simple and reliable: **the present moment**.

And when you keep returning to the present moment, you develop **resilience**.

Mindfulness is built through **repetition**. Each time you pause, notice your reaction, and return to the present moment, you strengthen the habit of responding with awareness rather than impulse.

For sure, some moments will be easier than others. There will still be times when you react quickly or become caught in stress before realizing it. But now you know that this is all part of the process.

Exercise 60: Your 3-Step Response Plan

This exercise helps you develop a **three-step response plan** you can return to when things go wrong.

Step 1: Pause

The first step is simply to pause. Instead of reacting immediately, give yourself a brief moment to stop and notice what's happening.

What helps you pause when stress appears?

Example: Freezing in place (because it reminds me I literally don't have to do anything in the next few seconds), closing my eyes, and taking a few deep breaths.

____

____

____

Step 2: Notice

After pausing, gently observe what is happening in your experience.

What thoughts are appearing?
What emotions are you feeling?
What is happening in your body?

What do you typically notice when stress appears?

Example: I notice that my shoulders are tense and my mind is racing with worst-case scenarios.

____

____

____

Step 3: Choose Your Response

Once you have paused and noticed what is happening, you can decide how you want to respond.

What response might help you stay steady in difficult moments?

Example: Time and space. I find that it helps if I step away and put some distance between what happened and what I should say or do next.

____

____

____

Step 4: Your 3-Step Reminder

If you can, write a few words describing your go-to 3-step response plan.

Example:
PAUSE: stop + breathe
NOTICE: do a quick body + emotion scan
RESPONSE: step away + return

PAUSE: _______________________________________

NOTICE: _______________________________________

RESPONSE: _______________________________________

Exercise 61: Mindfulness Compass

Throughout this book, you explored many different mindfulness skills:

- breathwork
- meditation
- deliberate pauses
- listening to your body
- practicing gratitude
- responding with self-compassion
- creating and implementing boundaries

Each person connects with these ideas in a slightly different way. This final activity helps you identify the mindfulness principles that feel most meaningful to you.

Think of them as a compass you can return to when life feels overwhelming, and as simple ways to strengthen your mindfulness practice.

Step 1: What Stood Out Most?

Looking back on the exercises and ideas in this book, which ones resonated with you the most?

Example: Learning to pause before reacting helped me the most. I was always "Go, go, go!" Now, I realize that's not always the best recourse.

____

____

____

____

____

Step 2: Your Personal Reminders

Write 3–5 simple reminders you would like to carry with you in daily life.

Example:
- *Pause before reacting.*
- *Breathe and return to the present.*
- *Check in with my body to see if I'm holding tension I'm not aware of.*
- *Pay it forward!*
- *Be kinder to myself.*

Your reminders:

1) ____

2) ____

3) ____

4) ____

5) ____

Step 3: When Will You Use Your Reminder?

Think about situations where you might need these reminders the most. Examples:

- stressful workdays
- difficult conversations

- moments of overwhelm
- when my mind starts racing
- during one of my predefined transition moments

____

____

____

____

____

Remember, mindfulness isn't about becoming perfectly calm or always getting things right. It's about remembering that **you can return to awareness, again and again**, no matter what is happening around you.

Your mindfulness compass will help guide you back.

Conclusion

Ah yes, the world can be loud, scary, and messy... but mindfulness changes something important: how you meet it.

Throughout this book, you explored small practices such as pausing before reacting, noticing signals in your body, interrupting mental spirals, appreciating small moments, and responding to yourself with compassion.

None of these practices is dramatic or complicated. In fact, as you may have noticed, most of them take only a few seconds. Yet together, they create something powerful.

They change how you move through your life.

When you practice mindfulness, you become less pulled by every thought, emotion, or stressful moment. You begin to notice what's happening without immediately becoming overwhelmed. You pause more often. You breathe. You respond with greater awareness.

These changes may feel small, but they ripple outward.

When you're calmer, your conversations become calmer.
When you respond with patience, tension often decreases.

When you bring presence into difficult moments, it subtly influences the people around you.

Mindfulness may not fix the world, but it changes the space you occupy within it.

And in a world that feels rushed and reactive, a mindful presence creates moments of steadiness, clarity, and kindness. Over time, these small moments accumulate.

You begin to notice that even in a messy world, there are still moments of calm, connection, humor, gratitude, and meaning. **Life remains imperfect, but the way you live it becomes lighter.**

So, let mindfulness be how you move through this world.

Each time you pause, breathe, and return to the present moment, you contribute something the world needs: a little more awareness, a little more steadiness, and a little more humanity.

Pay It Forward?

Hello. I sincerely hope something in this book helped you feel a little calmer, steadier, or more at ease in your day-to-day life. If it has, please consider leaving a short review on Amazon.

Reviews support authors like me, but more importantly, they help others who may be feeling overwhelmed, stressed, or disconnected find something that could support them too.

How to Help:
Step 1. Please visit this link
https://amazon.com/review/create-review?&asin=B0GX35TDWG or scan the QR code on this page.
Step 2. Share your thoughts about this book on Amazon. That's it!

Note: If you're from outside the US, please update the link above from amazon.com to your country code (e.g., amazon.co.uk, amazon.ca, amazon.de, etc.). Using Kindle or an e-reader? Scroll to the bottom of the book and swipe up to prompt the Review page.

THANK YOU FOR YOUR HELP!

Further Reading

Ready to turn these mindfulness practices into a daily habit?

The **2026 Mindfulness Journal** helps you carry what you've learned into your everyday life with simple, guided prompts. There's no need to wait for January 1—you can **begin anytime, right where you are**.

Get your copy here: https://amzn.to/4pkbjSA

About the Author

Ava Walters is the founder of LifeZen Publications. Coming from a family with a history of mental health issues, her journey began as a personal quest to find balance, inner peace, and what we all desire—happiness. This pursuit has led her to explore traditional psychotherapeutic methods and diverse holistic practices.

She has an MBA with a specialization in International Project Management (IPM). However, her trajectory took a significant turn after experiencing "burnout and a breakdown." She then returned to her first love, writing, complementing it with her deep passion for psychology. This transformation marked the beginning of her new journey. One focused on unraveling the intricate connections between human behavior and mental healing.

When she's not writing, Ava can be found on her yoga mat, taking long nature walks with her husband, or in the kitchen, constantly experimenting with new recipes to her husband's delight.

Learn more about Ava and LifeZen Publications here:
https://life-zen.com/

References

1 Wiens, K. (2025, January 13). *The insidious effects of hurrying.* Harvard Business Review. https://hbr.org/2025/01/the-insidious-effects-of-hurrying

2 Friedman, M., & Rosenman, R. H. (1992). *Type A behavior and your heart: The book for everyone who hopes to avoid heart attack.* Fawcett Crest.

3 Weierich, M. R., Wright, C. I., Negreira, A., Dickerson, B. C., & Barrett, L. F. (2010). Novelty as a dimension in the affective brain. *NeuroImage, 49*(3), 2871–2878. https://doi.org/10.1016/j.neuroimage.2009.09.047

4 Rossman, M. (2010). *The effects of stress on short-term and long-term memory.* Chancellor's Honors Program Projects. https://trace.tennessee.edu/utk_chanhonoproj/1342

5 Ackermann, S., Hartmann, F., Papassotiropoulos, A., de Quervain, D. J.-F., & Rasch, B. (2013). Associations between basal cortisol levels and memory retrieval in healthy young individuals. *Journal of Cognitive Neuroscience, 25*(11), 1896–1907. https://doi.org/10.1162/jocn_a_00440

6 More Perspectives from the frontline workforce | UKG. (2025). https://www.ukg.com/learn/resources/white-paper/more-perspectives-frontline-workforce

7 Masuda, A., Hayes, S. C., Sackett, C. F., & Twohig, M. P. (2004). Cognitive defusion and self-relevant negative thoughts: Examining the impact of a ninety year old technique. *Behaviour Research and Therapy, 42*(4), 477–485. https://doi.org/10.1016/j.brat.2003.10.008

8 Way, N., & Taffe, R. (2024). Interpersonal curiosity: A missing construct in the field of human development. *Human Development*, 1–12. https://doi.org/10.1159/000542162

9 Walters, A. (2025). *Somatic therapy workbook (just 10 mins a day): 70+ exercises to manage stress, Heal Trauma &... balance hormones - a somatic yoga & Breathwork*. Lifezen Publications.

10 Baddeley, B., Sornalingam, S., & Cooper, M. (2016). Sitting is the new smoking: Where do we stand? *British Journal of General Practice*, 66(646), 258–258. https://doi.org/10.3399/bjgp16x685009

11 Mayo Foundation for Medical Education and Research. (2025, March 26). *Sitting risks: How harmful is too much sitting?*. Mayo Clinic. https://www.mayoclinic.org/healthy-lifestyle/adult-health/expert-answers/sitting/faq-20058005

12 Department of Health & Human Services. (2016, August 8). *The dangers of sitting: Why sitting is the new smoking*. Better Health Channel. https://www.betterhealth.vic.gov.au/health/healthyliving/the-dangers-of-sitting

13 Mayo Foundation for Medical Education and Research. (2023, November 18). *Stretching: Focus on flexibility*. Mayo Clinic. https://www.mayoclinic.org/healthy-lifestyle/fitness/in-depth/stretching/art-20047931

14 Warneke, K., Thomas, E., Blazevich, A. J., Afonso, J., Behm, D. G., Marchetti, P. H., Trajano, G. S., Nakamura, M., Ayala, F., Longo, S., Babault, N., Freitas, S. R., Costa, P. B., Konrad, A., Nordez, A., Nelson, A., Zech, A., Kay, A. D., Donti, O., & Wilke, J. (2025). Practical recommendations on stretching exercise: A delphi consensus statement of international research experts. *Journal of Sport and Health Science*, 14, 101067. https://doi.org/10.1016/j.jshs.2025.101067

15 Lyubomirsky, S., Sheldon, K. M., & Schkade, D. (2005). Pursuing happiness: The Architecture of Sustainable Change. *Review of*

General Psychology, 9(2), 111–131.
https://doi.org/10.1037/1089-2680.9.2.111

16 Fowler, J. H., & Christakis, N. A. (2010). Cooperative behavior
cascades in human social networks. *Proceedings of the National
Academy of Sciences, 107*(12), 5334–5338.
https://doi.org/10.1073/pnas.0913149107